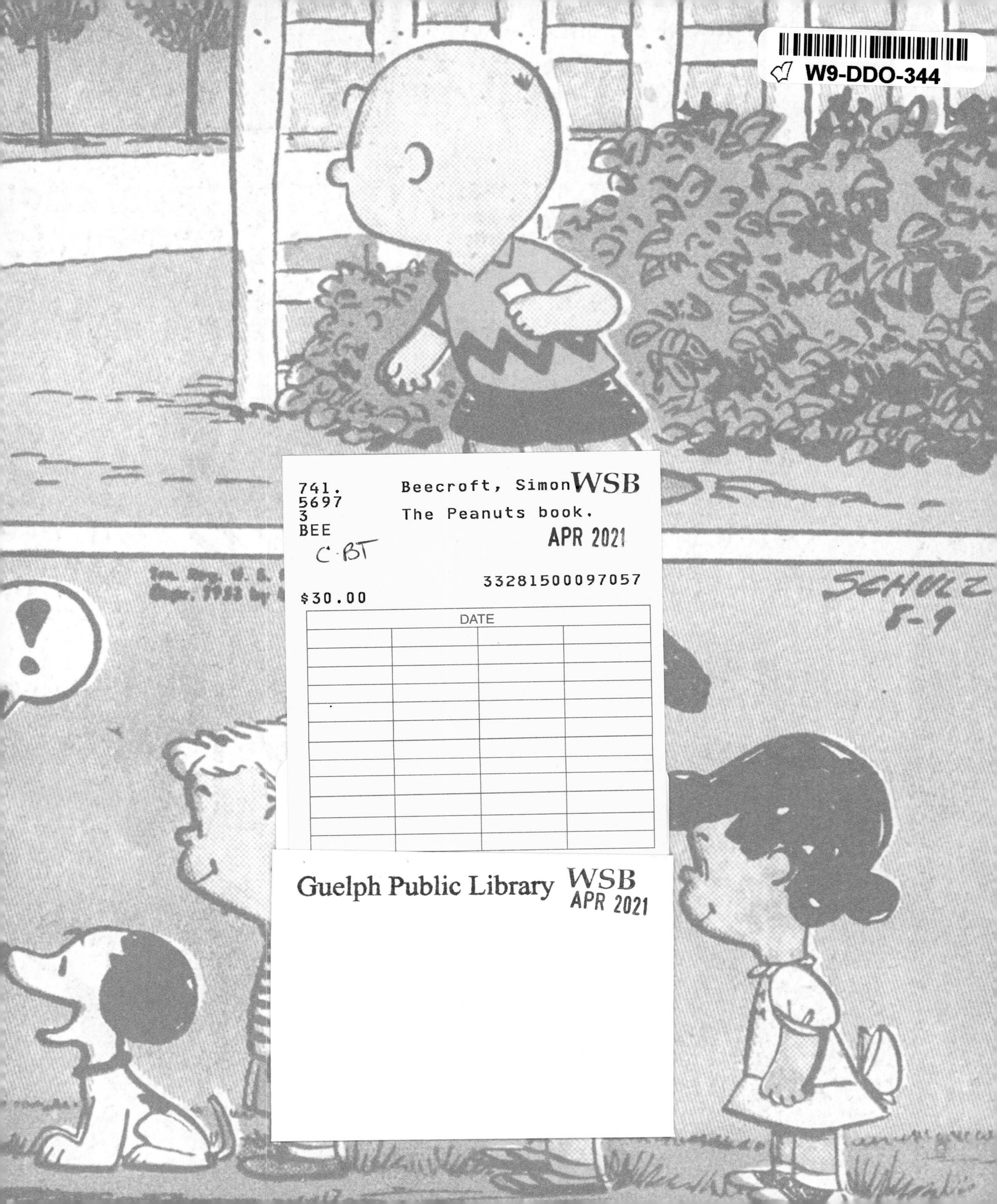
!
SCHULZ
8-9

THE PEANUTS™ BOOK

THE PEANUTS™ BOOK

A Visual History of the Iconic Comic Strip

Written by Simon Beecroft

Foreword by Stephen Colbert

DK

Contents

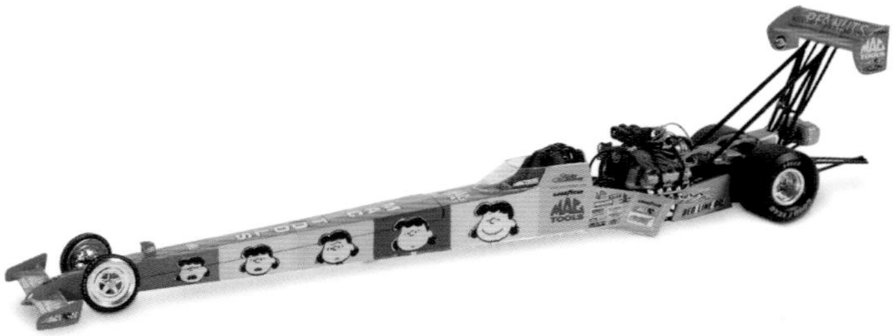

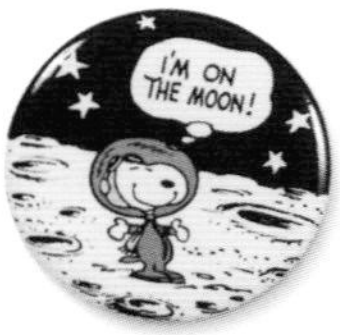

I'M ON THE MOON!

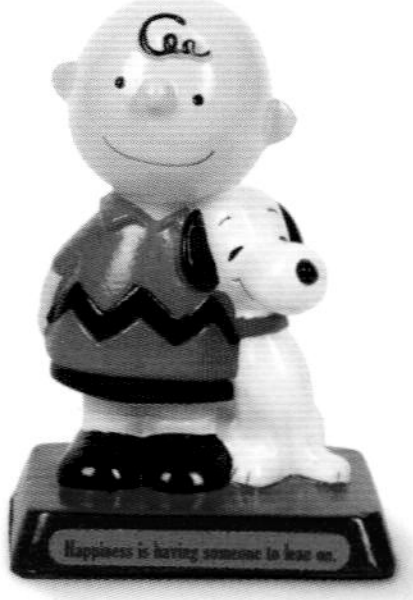

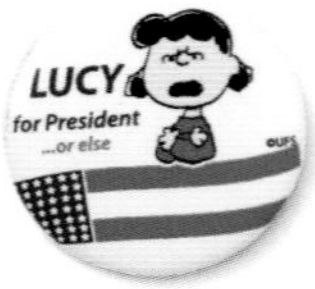

LUCY
for President
...or else

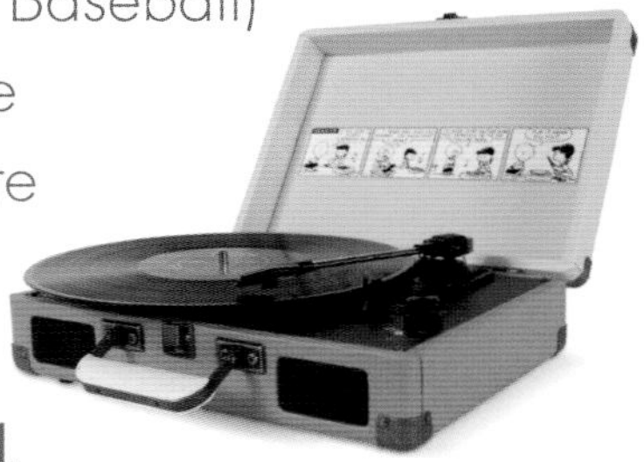

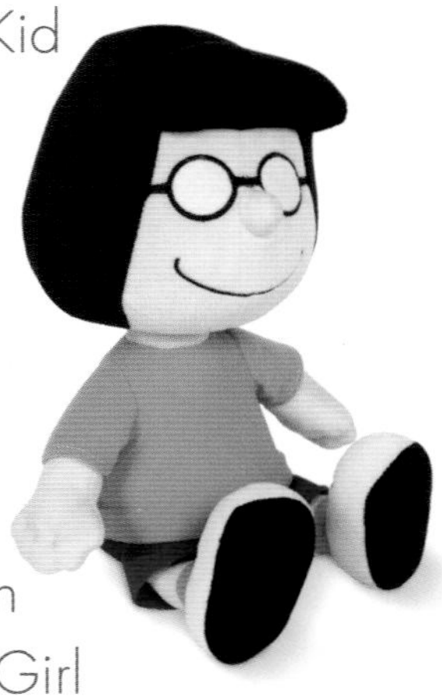

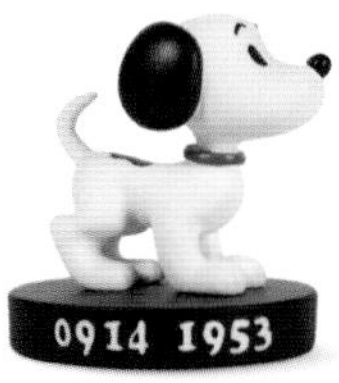
0914 1953
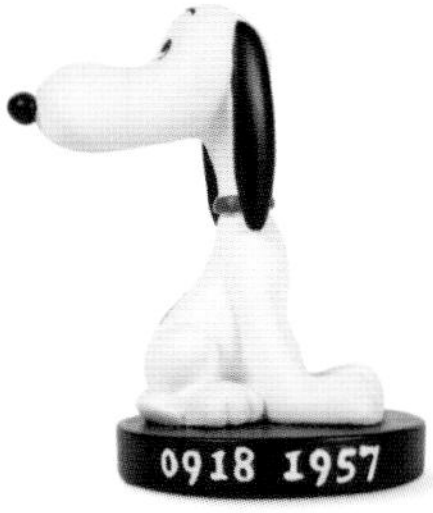
0918 1957
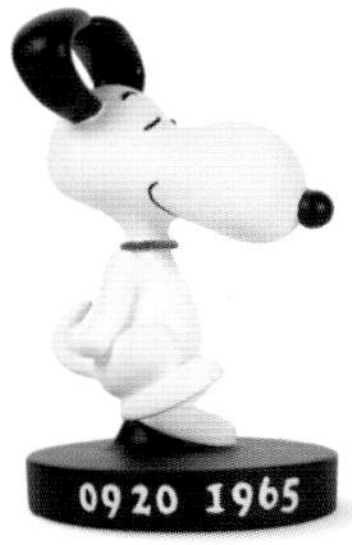
0920 1965
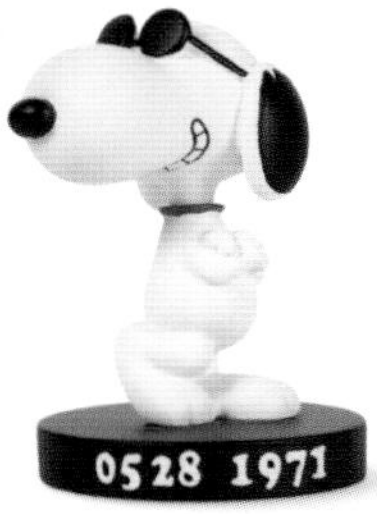
0528 1971
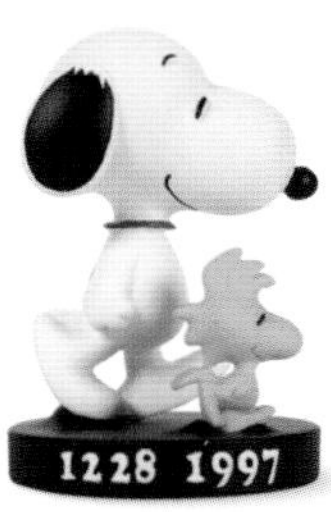
1228 1997

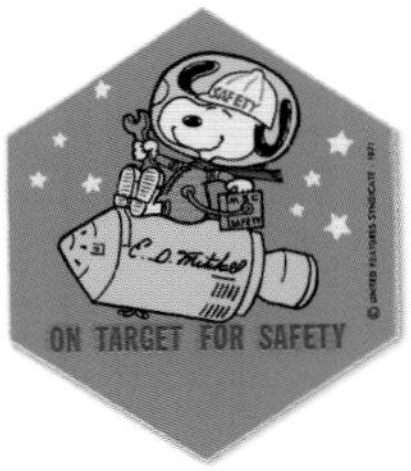
ON TARGET FOR SAFETY

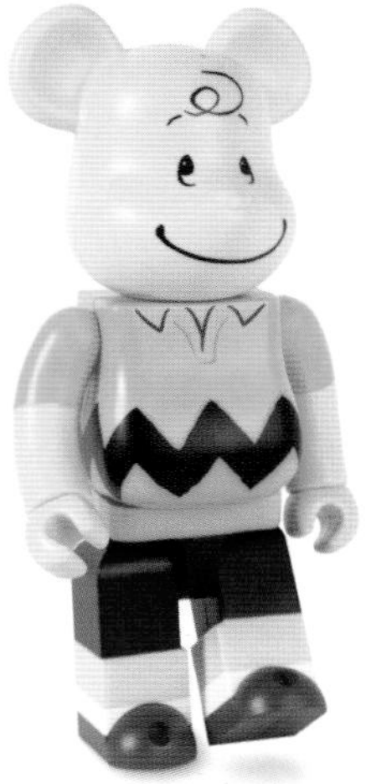

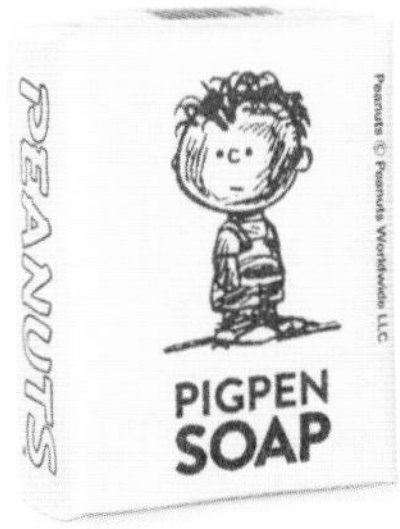
PEANUTS
PIGPEN
SOAP

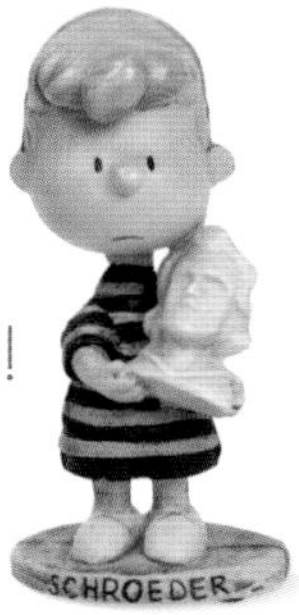
SCHROEDER

Foreword

have always loved *Peanuts*. I don't think I trust anyone who doesn't. So it's surprising that the last line of the very first strip was:

"Good Ol' Charlie Brown. How I hate him!"

Now, how could anyone hate Charlie Brown? But the choice is brilliant. From the beginning, Charles Schulz made it clear that *Peanuts*, while about children, was not going to be childish or simple or simply for children. It was going to be funny and sad and, best of all, funny about being sad. Or as Charlie Brown might say, "Good Grief." For 50 years, *Peanuts* was king of the comics page, and people of all ages read it every day, because Schulz knew that our inner lives as adults are rooted in our childhood wants and fears—emotions that we never fully leave behind. So, we recognize ourselves in the little victories and defeats of these *L'il Folks*. No matter how old we are, the tree will eat our kite. The little red-haired girl may never notice us. We get no Valentine's mail or Halloween candy. Our dog is more popular than we are. The football gets pulled away at the last minute, again. And again. But we know we will never give up trying. Every spring, we think this will be the winning season—blockheads to the end.

But in all this, Schulz, a man of deep faith, never points us toward despair. In that first strip, Charlie Brown strolls by the boy who hates him, as happy and oblivious as the Fool. Maybe he doesn't hear what Shermy says, or maybe he is just pretending he doesn't hear it. Either way, from the first strip to the last, Charlie Brown keeps walking on, forever a hero of hope.

Good Ol' Charlie Brown. How I love him!

Stephen Colbert

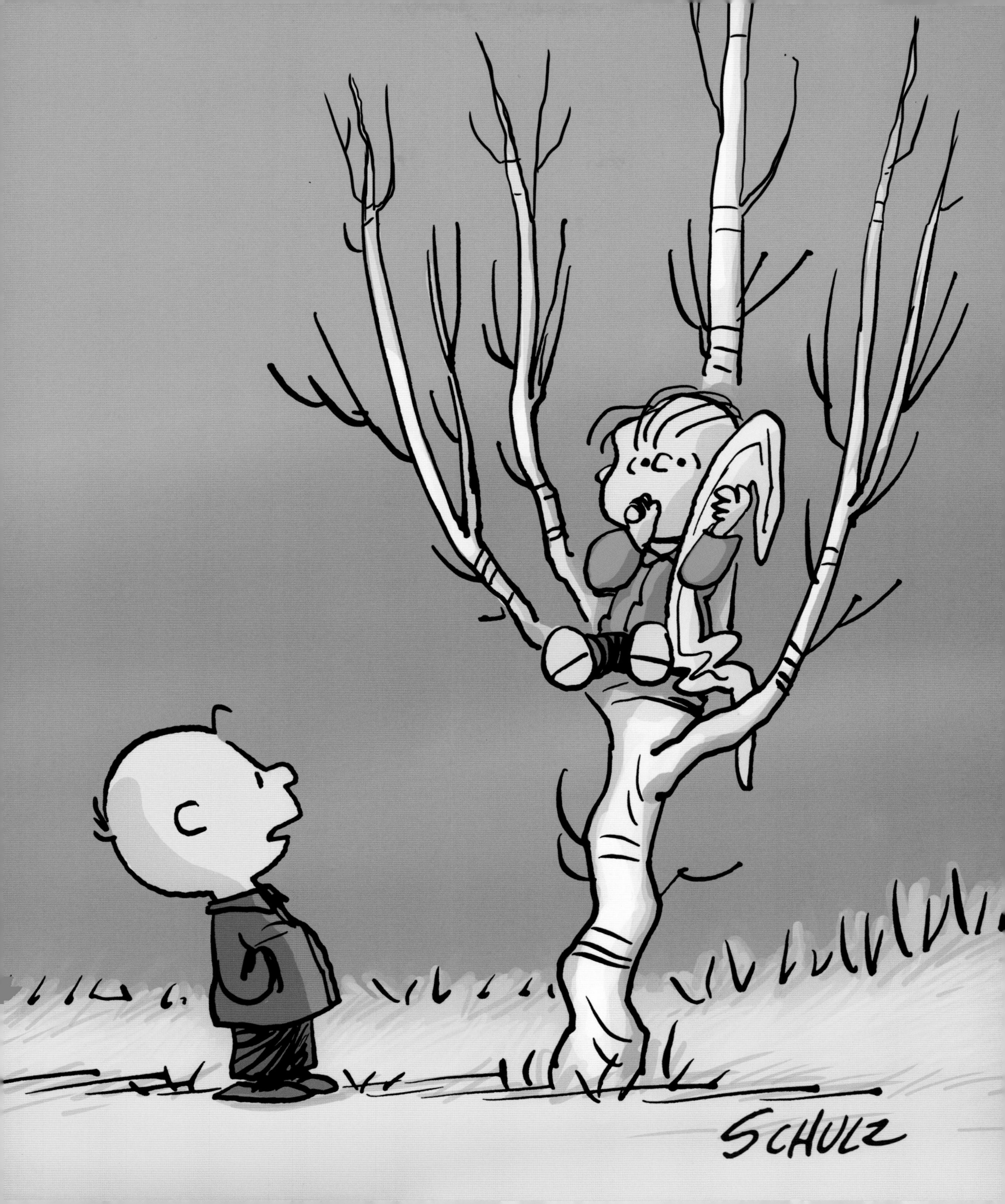
SCHULZ

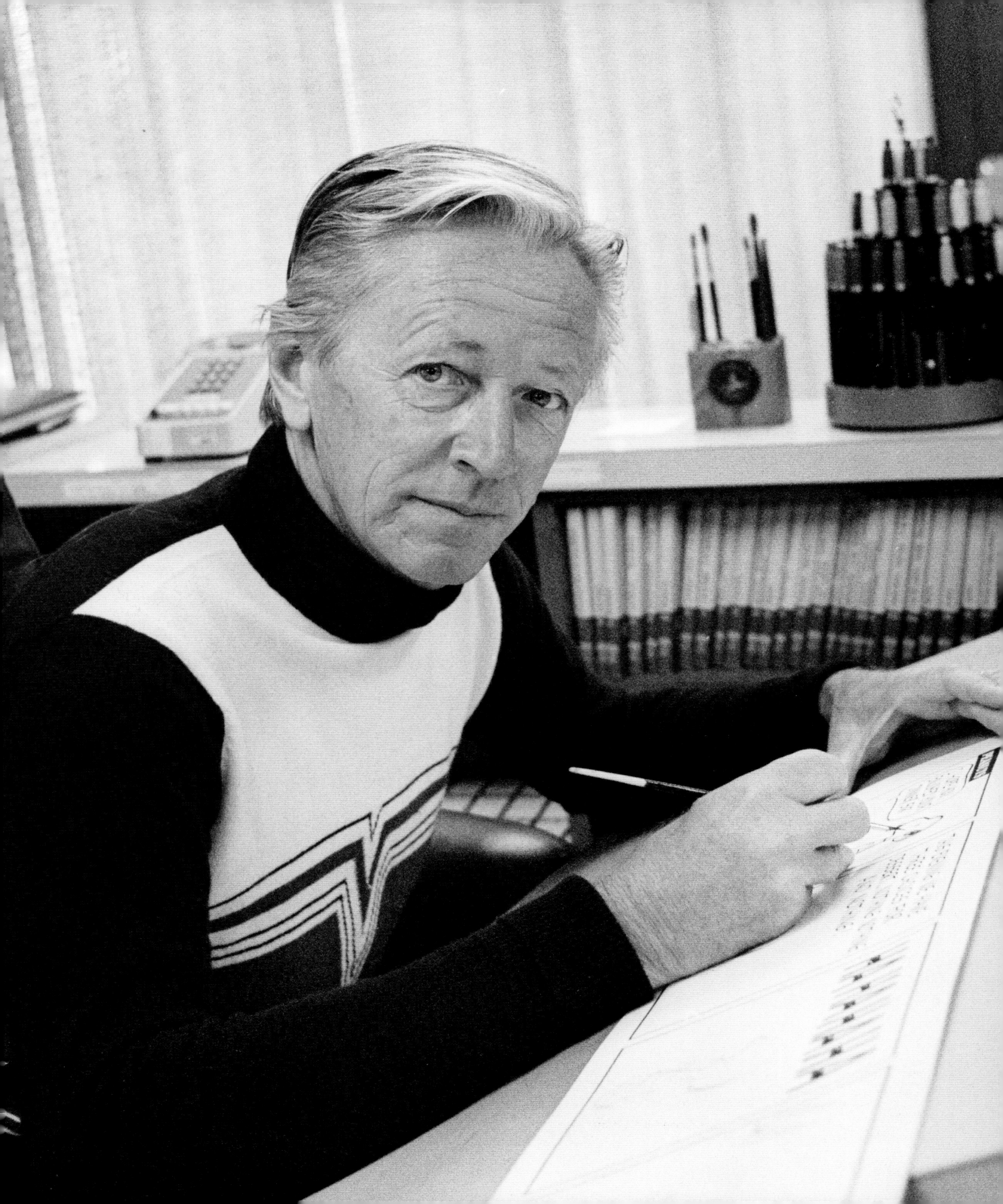

Introduction

The comic strip *Peanuts* means different things to different people: for some, it's all about the crazy antics of Snoopy and Woodstock; others will think of Charlie Brown and his gang of misfits, with their eccentricities and their problems; for many, it's the animated TV specials that appeared every holiday season (and still do), with the teacher who would say, "Wah wah wah." Everyone with even a passing familiarity with the strip will know some of its key tropes: Charlie Brown's "good grief" miserabilism, Linus's security blanket, Schroeder's piano, Snoopy's doghouse, Lucy's psychiatry stand. At its peak, the daily *Peanuts* comic strip was read by 355 million people in 21 languages across 75 countries. To those who grew up with *Peanuts*, it remains an indelible part of their makeup.

Peanuts is the creation of one man. Charles M. Schulz knew from boyhood that he had a destiny: "My ambition from earliest memory," he said, "was to produce a daily comic strip." Schulz single-handedly drew his daily strip for 50 years—his entire adult life—without assistants or stand-ins: a staggering total of 17,897 strips. He believed in the power of the comic strip as an art form and thought that it could convey any idea, emotion, or situation. From one day to the next, Schulz's strip could encompass wry humor, flat-out fun, social commentary, existential angst, psychological inquiry, philosophical reflection, and even theological debate.

◄ Snoopy is top dog in Japan. This book shows kids how to draw him and the gang.

Perhaps less well known is how much of the strip was inspired by events in Schulz's life and how personal the story he told was. "If you read the strip," Schulz said, "you would know me. Everything I am goes into the strip." Once described as the longest single story in history, *Peanuts* can be seen as Schulz's 50-year autobiography, featuring the many people who mattered in his life. In telling his story, he spoke for all of us, finding ways to express our fears and foibles, our need for friendship and love (and our frustration when we don't get it), and our insecurity when we aren't understood or heard.

This book explores the world of *Peanuts* in all its many forms, bringing together some wonderful visual material from the Charles M. Schulz Museum in Santa Rosa, California, some of which has never before been published. Showcased are original comic strips, preparatory sketches, and other artworks by Schulz—including drawings done when he was at school and in the army during World War II—along with evocative memorabilia from the 1950s to the present day. Starting with Schulz's early life in Minnesota during the Great Depression, we will see his single-minded pursuit of his dream to become a comic-strip artist. We will travel through five decades of *Peanuts*, discovering how its cast of characters expanded and changed and how Schulz found that there was little he couldn't say or do in his strip. Particularly fascinating is how Snoopy evolved from a cute little puppy to the world's wildest, most unpredictable cartoon character, a true global superstar. We will chart how *Peanuts* became an international brand, with its own theme parks, animated films, stage shows, toys, and collectibles, and even an ice rink! This book celebrates the plain ol' neighborhood that captures the imagination of children and adults like no other—and says so much to so many.

By Simon Beecroft

1920s to 1940s

Charles M. Schulz was raised during America's harshest economic downturn, the Great Depression, which lasted for 10 years beginning in 1929. From boyhood, he shared a love of comic strips with his father and had an ambition to draw one himself. With single-minded focus, Schulz pursued his dream and drew constantly through his youth and into young adulthood, where his first jobs post-war were in the field of art and cartooning.

1920
▶ May: Schulz's parents, Carl and Dena, marry in Minneapolis, Minnesota

1922
▶ November 26: Charles Monroe Schulz is born
▶ Two days after his birth, Schulz is nicknamed "Sparky" after a racehorse character, Spark Plug, in a newspaper comic strip.

1927
▶ The Schulzes move from Minneapolis to St. Paul, Minnesota, where Carl runs a barbershop named the Family Barbershop.

1929
▶ Schulz moves with his parents to Needles, California, "a little sandy town," according to him, and "a miserable place." They move back to St. Paul, Minnesota, just two years later.

1934
▶ Schulz's family is gifted a puppy named Spike, replacing their previous dog, Snooky, who was hit and killed by a taxicab. Spike would become the inspiration for Snoopy.
▶ At Richard Gordon Elementary School, Schulz is pronounced exceptionally bright and skips a grade; already a short child, his peers now tower over him; according to Schulz, "[I] got in over my head."

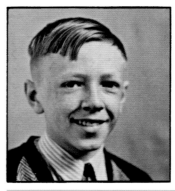

1937
▶ February 22: At age 14, Schulz's first published drawing, of his dog Spike, appeared in the newspaper feature *Ripley's Believe It or Not!*

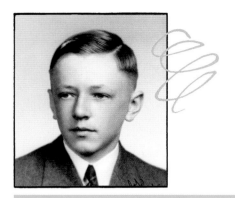

1940

► Schulz enrolls as home-study student in the Federal School of Applied Cartooning

1942

► November: Schulz receives his draft notice. In the same month, he discovers the true cause of his mother's debilitating illness: stage IV cancer of the cervix.

1943

► March: Schulz's mother dies; the day after her funeral, Schulz leaves for Camp Campbell on the border of Kentucky and Tennessee, where he spends two years training as a machine gunner.

1944

► September: Schulz is promoted to staff sergeant and leader of a light machine-gun squad

1945

► Schulz and his division ship out to France
► May: Germany surrenders
► July: Schulz returns to the United States

1946

► January: Schulz is discharged from the army and starts working at Art Instruction Inc. in Minneapolis (formerly called Federal School of Applied Cartooning), reviewing and grading home students' work.

1947

► February: Schulz's first appearance in print as a comic artist: a page of his cartoons appears under the banner *Just Keep Laughing* in *Topix*, a Catholic comic magazine; second page follows in April.
► June: *Li'l Folks* ("By Sparky"), Schulz's first weekly feature, debuts in the *St. Paul Pioneer Press*
► Schulz rejects an offer of a one-month tryout at Walt Disney Studios in Los Angeles

1948

► Schulz's first major sale: a spot cartoon to the *Saturday Evening Post* for $40

1949

► Schulz starts dating Donna Mae Johnson, who will eventually marry someone else. Schulz will later immortalize her in *Peanuts* as Charlie Brown's great unrequited love, the Little Red-Haired Girl.

1950s

S chulz's first strip, *Li'l Folks*, ended its run in January 1950. On October, 2, 1950, his new strip, *Peanuts*, debuted. The first decade of the strip saw its major characters established: Charlie Brown, Lucy, Linus, Schroeder, Snoopy, and Sally. Many of the strip's major themes were also introduced, including Lucy holding the football for Charlie Brown, Snoopy's happy dance, Lucy's psychiatry booth, Charlie Brown's baseball team, Linus's security blanket and the Great Pumpkin, and Schroeder's piano. By the end of the decade the strip was established across the United States and beyond.

1950

▶ January 22: Final *Li'l Folks* panel appears in *St. Paul Pioneer Press*

▶ October 2: *Peanuts* debuts in seven newspapers; Charlie Brown, Patty, and Shermy introduced; first use of "Good ol' Charlie Brown"

▶ October 4: First appearance of Snoopy

▶ December 21: Charlie Brown first appears in zigzag shirt

1951

▶ February 7: Violet's first appearance

▶ March 6: The gang's first baseball game

▶ April 18: Schulz and Joyce Steele Halverson are married. Soon afterward, Schulz adopts Joyce's one-year-old daughter, Meredith, from a previous, short-lived marriage.

▶ May: Charles Schulz and his family move to Colorado Springs, Colorado

▶ May 30: Schroeder's first appearance (as a baby)

▶ August 16: Charlie Brown is first called a "blockhead" (by Violet)

▶ September 4: Snoopy's doghouse first appears

▶ September 24: Schroeder's piano first appears

▶ November 14: Charlie Brown first tries to kick a football (held by Violet)

▶ November 26: Schroeder expresses his love of Beethoven for the first time

1952

▶ January 6: First full-color *Peanuts* Sunday strip appears

▶ February 1: The Schulzes' first son, Charles Monroe ("Monte"), is born

▶ March: The Schulz family moves back to Minneapolis, Minnesota

▶ March 3: Lucy's first appearance (as a toddler)

▶ March 21: Charlie Brown first tries to fly a kite

▶ May 27: Snoopy's first thought balloon

▶ July 1: First *Peanuts* book collection is published

▶ September 19: Linus's first appearance (as a baby)

▶ November 16: Lucy first holds a football for Charlie Brown

1953

▶ January 22: The Schulzes' second son, Craig Frederick, is born

▶ April 13: Lucy is first called a "fussbudget"

▶ May 13: Lucy falls in love with Schroeder

▶ December 16: Schroeder first celebrates Beethoven's birthday

1954

▶ January 17: Linus speaks for the first time

▶ June 1: Linus's security blanket first appears

▶ July 13: Pigpen's first appearance

▶ November 30: Charlotte Braun's first appearance

1955

▶ February 1: Final appearance of Charlotte Braun

▶ March 25: Snoopy first grabs Linus's blanket

1956

▶ January: Kodak becomes first product sponsor for *Peanuts*, using Schulz's characters in a booklet demonstrating popular photography techniques, which comes with Brownie cameras

▶ January 9: Snoopy ice-skates on a pond for the first time

▶ April: The National Cartoonists Society votes Schulz the outstanding cartoonist of 1955

▶ April 12: Charlie Brown first gets his kite stuck in a tree

▶ August 5: The Schulzes' daughter Amy Louise is born

▶ September 27: Snoopy first does his "happy dance"

▶ November 20: First appearance of Charlie Brown's "thinking wall"

1957

▶ June 28: Charlie Brown "teaches" Snoopy to walk on two legs

▶ October 14: Linus first tries to give up his blanket

▶ November 3: Schulz's sports-themed strip, called *It's Only a Game*, first appears in 28 newspapers

1958

▶ The first *Peanuts* character dolls are produced by Hungerford Plastics Corporation

▶ April 20: The Schulzes' fifth child, Jill Marie, is born

▶ May 13: Snoopy first poses as a vulture

▶ June: Schulz family leaves Minnesota and moves to Coffee Lane, Sebastopol, California

▶ August 25: Charlie Brown first writes to his pen pal (called his "pencil-pal")

▶ November 23: The cat next door is first mentioned

▶ December 12: Snoopy sleeps on top of his doghouse for the first time

1959

▶ March 27: Lucy opens her psychiatry booth

▶ May 26: Sally is born

▶ August 23: Sally's first appearance (as a baby)

▶ October 5: Linus falls in love with his teacher, Miss Othmar

▶ October 26: Linus first mentions the Great Pumpkin

▶ November: Ford Motor Company licenses the *Peanuts* gang to advertise their new model, the *Falcon*

1960s

The strip sees new iconic characters introduced, including Snoopy's World War I Flying Ace and Peppermint Patty. *Peanuts* makes the cover of *Time* magazine, and Schulz wins an unprecedented second major award from the National Cartoonists Society. Now at the height of his fame, Schulz oversees the expansion of the strip into merchandise, advertising sponsorships, TV specials, a movie and stage show, and official endorsement by NASA.

1960

▶ Hallmark issues the first *Peanuts* greetings cards

▶ March 14: Snoopy spins his ears like a helicopter for the first time

▶ March 21: Linus's blanket-hating grandmother is first mentioned

▶ April 25: Lucy hugs Snoopy and says, "Happiness is a warm puppy," a phrase that will go on to spawn a popular merchandise craze

▶ August 22: Sally walks for the first time (and falls in love with Linus)

1961

▶ March 6: First appearance of Frieda, "the girl with naturally curly hair"

▶ May 4: First appearance of Lucy's psychiatry booth with the DOCTOR IS IN sign

▶ May 23: First appearance of Frieda's cat, Faron

▶ May 31: Sally says her first words

▶ November 19: The Little Red-Haired Girl is first mentioned

1962

▶ *Peanuts* is named Best Humor Strip of the Year by the National Cartoonists Society

▶ February 5: Linus wears glasses for the first time

▶ September 5: Sally starts kindergarten

▶ September 9: Linus appears in glasses for the last time

▶ October 1: *Happiness Is a Warm Puppy* book is published by Determined Productions

1963

▶ March 13: Snoopy first interacts with the notes from Schroeder's piano

▶ July 6: Sally states that Snoopy is a beagle

▶ August 18: First reference to Joe Shlabotnik, Charlie Brown's favorite baseball player

▶ September 30: First appearance of "5" (full name: 555 95472)

▶ October 17: First appearance of 5's siblings, "3" and "4"

1964

▶ Schulz wins unprecedented second Reuben Award from the National Cartoonists Society

▶ January 21: Sally first struggles with a book report

1965

▶ March 14: The Kite-Eating Tree is named for the first time

▶ April: Charlie Brown and the gang appear on the cover of *Time* magazine

▶ May 4: Snoopy first refers to his birthplace, the Daisy Hill Puppy Farm

▶ May 5: Snoopy first mentions his brothers and sisters

▶ June 5: Charlie Brown first goes to camp

▶ June 11: Roy's first appearance

▶ July 12: Snoopy debuts as "the great author," with the immortal first sentence, "It was a dark and stormy night."

▶ October 10: Snoopy first appears as the World War I Flying Ace

▶ November 29: Sally is tested for amblyopia (lazy eye) and must wear an eye patch

▶ December 9: *A Charlie Brown Christmas* debuts (wins an Emmy and a Peabody Award in 1966)

1966

▶ March 4: First appearance of (unnamed) Woodstock

▶ May 9: Lucy and Linus have to move away (but return within a week)

▶ May 29: Schulz's father, Carl, passes away

▶ May 31: Sally's lazy eye is cured, and she gives her eye patch to Snoopy the pirate

▶ August 22: Peppermint Patty's first appearance

▶ August 29: Peppermint Patty first calls Snoopy a "funny-looking kid"

▶ September 19: Snoopy's doghouse burns to the ground (earlier that same year, Schulz's art studio burned down)

1967

▶ March 7: *You're a Good Man, Charlie Brown* opens off-Broadway and runs for four years; during which the stage musical also opens in other cities.

▶ March 17: Charlie Brown and Snoopy appear on the cover of *Life* magazine

▶ March 20: José Peterson's first appearance

▶ April 18: Snoopy first does his "Cheshire Beagle" trick (vanishing down to his smile)

▶ May 24: The California Legislative Assembly declares "Charles Schulz Day" in honor of his success with *Peanuts*

1968

▶ NASA uses Snoopy in the Manned Flight Awareness Program and on the Silver Snoopy pin (given for good safety records)

▶ January 27: Charlie Brown first visits his father's barbershop

▶ February 17: First mention of Snoopy's first owner, Lila

▶ June 18: First appearance of Peppermint Patty's tent wards, Sophie, Clara, and Shirley

▶ July 31: First appearance of Franklin

▶ November 28: First *Peanuts* character balloon at Macy's Thanksgiving Day Parade in New York City

1969

▶ April 28: The Redwood Empire Ice Arena ("Snoopy's Home Ice") opens in Santa Rosa, California

▶ May 18: NASA's Apollo 10 command and lunar modules, named *Charlie Brown* and *Snoopy*, orbit the Moon

▶ September 9: First mention of the Head Beagle

▶ December 4: *A Boy Named Charlie Brown* debuts in movie theaters

1970s

Schulz's marriage to Joyce comes to an end and the cartoonist finds new everlasting love with Jean, embracing an active lifestyle of tennis and jogging. The popularity of the strip continues to surge, with new characters including Woodstock, Marcie, and Snoopy's brother Spike. *Peanuts* celebrates its 25th anniversary in 1975.

1970

► February 16: Snoopy is promoted to Head Beagle (an event honored by the mayor of Los Angeles with a specially made congratulatory certificate)

► June 4: First appearance of Thibault

► June 13: Snoopy first appears as Joe Cool (unnamed)

► June 22: Woodstock is named for the first time

1971

► May 27: First named appearance of Snoopy's alter ego, Joe Cool

► June 17: Peanuts Day is declared in San Diego, California

► July 7: Sally first talks to the school building

► July 20: First appearance of Marcie

1972

► May 23: Linus and Lucy's brother Rerun is born

► July 14: *Snoopy, Come Home* debuts in movie theaters

► December: Charles and Joyce Schulz divorce after more than 20 years of marriage

1973

► March 26: Rerun makes first appearance

► June 23: Charlie Brown is elected camp president as Mr. Sack

► September 22: Marriage of Charles Schulz and Jean ("Jeannie") Forsyth

1974

► January 21: Rerun first appears on his mother's bicycle

► March 21: Peppermint Patty learns that Snoopy is a dog and not a funny-looking kid

1975

▶ May 13: Snoopy becomes a Beagle Scout

▶ May 22: First appearance of cookie-selling Girl Scout Loretta

▶ May 28: TV special *A Charlie Brown Thanksgiving* wins Emmy award, after first airing November 20, 1973

▶ June 9: Woodstock and his bird friends become Beagle Scouts

▶ July 31–August 5: Schulz appears at San Diego Comic-Con for the first and only time

▶ September 6: Sally and the school building fall in love

▶ January: *Peanuts* celebrates its 25th anniversary with a TV special and a birthday note from President Gerald Ford

1976

1977

▶ March 31: First appearance of Linus and Snoopy's heartthrob, Truffles

▶ August 13: First appearance of Snoopy's desert-dwelling brother Spike

▶ June 28: First appearance of Snoopy's sister, Belle

▶ July 26: First appearance of Floyd at summer camp with Peppermint Patty and Marcie

▶ October 20: "The Cat Next Door" is named "World War II" for the first time

▶ January 27: Sally first calls Linus her "Sweet Babboo" (a term of endearment used by Jean for Schulz)

▶ March 11: Charlie Brown first meets Austin and Ruby from the Goose Eggs

1978

▶ March 17: First appearance of Leland from the Goose Eggs

▶ March 18: First appearance of Milo from the Goose Eggs

▶ May 9: First appearance of argumentative tennis player Molly Volley

▶ August 9: Snoopy decides to get married, with Spike as his best man

▶ August 25: Spike runs off with Snoopy's bride-to-be

▶ June 13: First appearance of Sally's friend Eudora

▶ July 5: First appearance of doubles tennis player "Crybaby" Boobie

1980s

The 1980s sees Schulz set a new record: the only cartoonist to have his strip appearing in 2,000 newspapers (and counting!). His characters are universally known and loved, and Schulz becomes the elder statesman of comics. He still creates the strip himself, without—as many successful cartoonists have—a team of assistants.

1980

▶ Schulz wins the Elzie Segar Award (named for the creator of the cartoon strip *Popeye*), presented by the National Cartoonists Society for "outstanding contributions to the art of cartooning"

1981

▶ June 22: First appearance of snooty golfer Joe Richkid

▶ September 2: Schulz has heart bypass surgery; afterward, he takes up jogging

1982

▶ April 15: First appearance of doubles tennis player "Bad Call" Benny

▶ September 28 : First appearance of Snoopy's brother Marbles

1983

▶ March 14: Peppermint Patty's baseball team's name is revealed to be the Pelicans

▶ June 30: Bill and Harriet, from Snoopy's Beagle Scouts, get married

▶ July 1: The first Camp Snoopy opens at Knott's Berry Farm, Buena Park, California

▶ September 17: *The Charlie Brown and Snoopy Show* debuts on CBS

▶ September 20: *Snoopy: The Musical* opens in London at the West End's Duchess Theatre

▶ December 24: First appearance of Sally's friend Harold Angel

1984

▶ *Peanuts* now appears in 2,000 newspapers and wins a place in the *Guinness Book of World Records*

▶ May 25: *Snoopy in Fashion* exhibition opens at Fashion Institute of Technology in New York

▶ September: The first annual Woodstock Open Golf Tournament is held in Santa Rosa, California

▶ December: *Snoopy in Fashion* exhibition opens in Tokyo

1985

▶ January: *The Graphic Art of Charles Schulz* exhibit, celebrating 35 years of *Peanuts,* opens in Oakland Museum of California

1986

▶ June 9: First appearance of Linus's young friend Lydia

▶ July 21: First appearance of Peppermint Patty's tutor, Maynard

▶ September 4: First appearance of Charlie Brown and Linus's classmate Tapioca Pudding

▶ October 13: Sally states her first philosophy

▶ November: Schulz is awarded the Santa Rosa Key to the City for public service

▶ December: *Snoopy's Wonderful Magical Christmas*, the first ice show at the Redwood Empire Ice Arena, opens

1987

▶ Schulz is inducted into Cartoonist Hall of Fame by the Museum of Cartoon Art

▶ January 4: Last Sunday strip to bear the tagline "featuring 'Good ol' Charlie Brown'"

▶ January 11: New *Peanuts* logo first used on Sunday strip

1988

▶ February 29: Daily strip goes to standard size and ends its strict four-frame format, starting various panel layouts

1989

▶ January 19: First appearance of Snoopy's brother Olaf

▶ June 18: Snoopy's father appears

▶ December: Schulz travels to Paris to receive the prestigious Commandeur de l'Ordre des Artes et des Lettres from the French Ministry of Culture

1990s to Present

As the only cartoonist to receive the honor of an exhibition of his work at the Louvre Museum in Paris, Schulz's place in the history books is confirmed by the 1990s. Despite his shaky wrist, he soldiered on, giving us Charlie Brown's only-ever wins at baseball, a first sighting of the Little Red-Haired Girl (in silhouette), and a new sibling for Snoopy (fuzzy-furred Andy). He officially retired from the strip on December 14, 1999.

1990
▶ January: *Snoopy in Fashion* exhibit opens at the Louvre Museum, Paris, France.

▶ July 23: First appearance of Charlie Brown's girlfriend, Peggy Jean

1992
▶ *Snoopy, the Masterpiece* exhibition opens in the Montreal Museum of Fine Arts

▶ August: Camp Snoopy opens at the Mall of America, Bloomington, Minnesota

▶ October: Schulz travels to Italy to receive the Order of Merit from the Italian Minister of Culture

1993
▶ March 30: Charlie Brown finally leads his baseball team to victory

▶ April 1: First appearance of baseball player Royanne Hobbs

1994
▶ September 27: Charlie Brown learns that his pen pal is a Scottish girl named Morag

1995
▶ February 11: First appearance of Charlie Brown's dance partner, Emily

▶ April 7: First appearance of marbles player (and bully) Joe Agate

1996
▶ June: Schulz receives his star on the Hollywood Walk of Fame

▶ July 26: Snoopy's mother appears

▶ September 11: First appearance of Rerun's friend, the (unnamed) Little Pigtailed Girl

1997

▶ March: World premiere of *Peanuts Gallery*, by Schulz's friend, composer Ellen Taaffe Zwilich, at Carnegie Hall, New York. The six-movement piano concerto celebrated favorite characters from the strip.

1998

▶ May 25: The Little Red-Haired Girl is seen in silhouette

▶ October 1: First appearance of Spike's friend Naomi

1999

▶ May: Camp Snoopy opens at the Cedar Point amusement park in Ohio

▶ July 11: Peggy Jean breaks up with Charlie Brown

▶ December 14: Schulz announces his retirement in an open letter

2000

▶ January 3: The final *Peanuts* daily strip appears

▶ February 12: Schulz dies peacefully in his sleep at home

▶ February 13: The final *Peanuts* Sunday strip appears

▶ May: 600 members of the National Cartoonists Society and guests honor Schulz posthumously with the Milton Caniff Lifetime Achievement Award, accepted on his behalf by Jean Schulz

▶ June: United States Congress posthumously awards Schulz with the highest civilian honor, the Congressional Gold Medal

2002

▶ August: The Charles M. Schulz Museum and Research Center opens

2012

▶ March: Snoopy Studios opens at Universal Studios, Japan

2015

▶ October 19: *The Peanuts Movie* is released in movie theaters in 3D CGI animation

2020

▶ October: *Peanuts* celebrates its 70th anniversary

"It seems beyond the comprehension of people that someone can be born to draw comic strips, but I think I was."

—Charles M. Schulz

Born to Draw

Meet Schulz

Charles M. Schulz enjoyed fame in sunny California, but he started out in a much colder climate. Born in 1922 and raised in Minnesota, he was the only child of Carl Schulz and Dena Halverson. From a young age, Schulz loved drawing and decided that he was going to draw comic strips for a living. It took many years of hard work and countless rejection slips, but eventually Schulz realized his dream, becoming one of the world's most famous comic strip artists.

BOYHOOD
Schulz lived through the Great Depression, though his mind was more on baseball, ice-skating, and, of course, drawing. He did well at school and was moved up a grade, making him the youngest and smallest in his year. He never forgot the feelings of shyness he felt from that time.

BELOVED PARENTS
Schulz was close to his parents. His mother encouraged Schulz's artistic ambitions when she called his attention to an ad for drawing classes, which he took. His mother died of cancer after a long illness in 1943, shortly after Schulz joined the army. Schulz's father was a barber, and Schulz admired his stoic work ethic, a trait he carried into his own daily routine as a comic strip artist.

NOTABLE NICKNAME
Shortly after Schulz was born, an uncle visited and pronounced that he should be called "Sparky," after Spark Plug, a then-popular racehorse character from a newspaper comic strip. The name stuck throughout his life.

"I think it was an advantage for me and my work being brought up in the Midwest because you get a view of the way people live."
—Charles M. Schulz

GROWING FAMILY

Schulz married his first wife, Joyce Halverson (no relation to his mother Dena Halverson Schulz) in 1951, a year after the *Peanuts* strip had started to run. Joyce already had a one-year-old daughter from a previous relationship whom Schulz adopted, and together they had four more children—whose early antics influenced gags in *Peanuts*.

LATE LOVE

At the age of 50, Schulz, recently divorced, married Jean Clyde, whom he met at his ice rink in Santa Rosa (named Snoopy's Home Ice). Sporty and devoted to Schulz, "Jeannie" would inspire much tennis-playing in the strip, as well as Sally's phrase "Sweet Babboo," which she was known to call Schulz.

COFFEE LANE

In 1958, in the first flush of his success, Schulz moved the family from Minnesota to California. Schulz bought a large house on Coffee Lane, in Sebastopol, California, where Joyce masterminded the construction of a private Disneyland, with heated pool, tennis court, miniature golf course, hedge maze, four-story tree house, and much more.

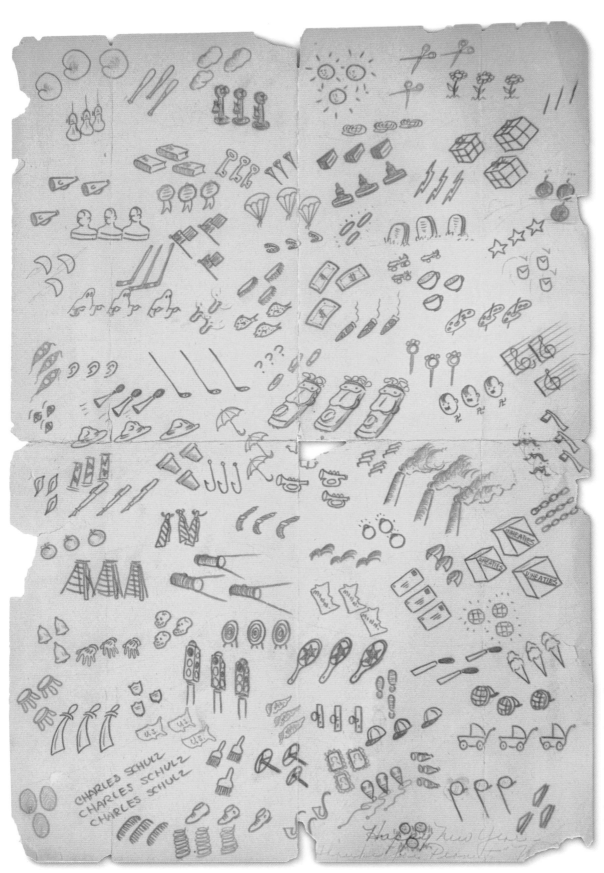

TEENAGE INGENUITY

The original sheets of high school art-class drawings, which Schulz's art teacher, Miss Paro, sent back to him, are inscribed by her in the bottom right corner.

Drawing of Threes

In 1938, when Schulz was 16 years old, his high school teacher Minette Paro gave her students a drawing assignment. They were to take a 12-by-18-inch (30-by-47-cm) sheet of drawing paper and draw anything they could think of, in sets of three. Some of the students struggled to complete three drawings of even one object. Schulz managed to fill his entire sheet in less than five minutes. He drew dozens of everyday objects rendered as cartoon icons: light bulbs, baseball bats, bullhorns, flashlights, traffic lights, doorknobs, barber poles, dollar bills, cereal boxes, and many more. He even drew three Adolf Hitlers (the United Kingdom and France would declare war on Nazi Germany in 1939), as well as something that was not then an icon, but would become one: his own name, CHARLES SCHULZ. Miss Paro was impressed and held up his picture as an example to the rest of the class. She said the drawings were "spectacular because they were things you wouldn't even think of … his mind was working every minute." Twenty-five years later she sent the original drawing to Schulz in the post. "Happy New Year," she wrote. "And thanks for 'Peanuts.'"

"It is interesting today to look back at that project and to see how I was affected by the times and by what was going on in my life."
—Charles M. Schulz

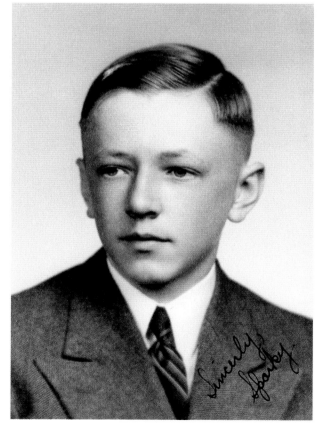

SENIOR YEAR
In his senior year, Schulz's mother showed him an advertisement for correspondence drawing classes with Federal Schools, Inc. (later known as Art Instruction, Inc.) His parents enrolled him in the spring of 1940, setting him on the road to his career as a cartoonist.

Li'l Folks

Schulz was no overnight success, but the single-minded pursuit of his dream eventually paid off with his first regular weekly strip: *Li'l Folks.*

▲ Schulz's time in World War II made a huge impression on him. Promoted to staff sergeant, he was responsible for a group of soldiers, and this bolstered his confidence.

After graduating from high school, Schulz had several jobs, including caddying at his local golf course. In his spare time, he was always drawing. In 1943, his mother died of cancer. Schulz barely had time to grieve: he had been called up by the US Army to serve in France during World War II. In 1946, he was discharged and resumed living at home with his father. He began working as an instructor at Art Instruction Inc. (formerly Federal Schools), the correspondence school where he had trained.

BREAKTHROUGH

In 1946, he found his first paid professional work, lettering comic book stories. Though it wasn't drawing, Schulz put his heart into it and his dedication paid off. Soon the editor of the comic ran two pages of Schulz's own cartoons under the heading *Just Keep Laughing.* The following year, Schulz managed to sell a weekly feature to the *St. Paul Pioneer Press.* Called *Li'l Folks,* it ran for two and a half years. The strip included early versions of Charlie Brown and a dog who resembled Snoopy. There was even a kid who loved Beethoven and a boy who liked to roll in the dirt. As in *Peanuts,* no adults were ever seen.

NATIONAL PUBLICATION

Around the same time, Schulz had his first sale to a mainstream magazine: a cartoon of a boy sitting at the end of a chaise longue—with his feet propped up on a footstool. He sent it unsolicited to the *Saturday Evening Post* and received a reply: "Check Tuesday for spot drawing of boy on lounge," which he took to mean his drawing had been

◀ Schulz drew vignettes of army life in a red-covered sketchbook that he entitled "As We Were." His impressions of war would stay with him throughout his life.

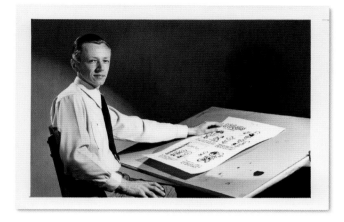

◄ Schulz's *Just Keep Laughing* pages featured children, adults, and even bugs. One of these cartoons showed little kids talking in an unusually grown-up way—a sign of what was to come.

▲ Schulz at his drawing desk with a completed page of *Li'l Folks*. This particular page would run on May 2, 1948.

rejected and would be sent back in the mail on Tuesday. In fact, the drawing had been accepted, and he received a check for $40 (on Tuesday!). This was the first of 17 cartoons that Schulz sold to the same publication.

MOVING ON

With his work now appearing in two publications, Schulz felt that *Li'l Folks* should become a daily feature. His request was denied, and he decided then and there to quit. None of the work he had done on *Li'l Folks* would be wasted—his next big breakthrough was just around the corner.

▲ *Li'l Folks* features a variety of children expressing adult sentiments and neurotic tendencies (and an obsession with Beethoven), as well as a dog who questions his place in the universe. Schulz would develop these themes much further in *Peanuts*.

► This cartoon, from May 1949, features the first mention of a character called Charlie Brown, with the almost-identical line to the very first *Peanuts* strip. Already, Schulz is focused on small children making grown-up, occasionally cruel, observations.

▲ Working at Art Instruction Inc. allowed Schulz (*perched on a desk, center back*) to develop cartoons with an audience in mind, showing sketches to colleagues to witness their reaction. The encouragement he received when he drew his little-kid cartoons inspired him to keep on going.

Origins of *Peanuts*

Schulz begins work on a new strip featuring little kids with large heads, often being "very nasty to each other."

Still working at Art Instruction Inc., Schulz had set his sights on selling a strip to a newspaper syndicate. Syndicates operate as agents for writers and cartoonists, placing their work in as many newspapers as possible. But competition to get represented was fierce. Schulz aimed to stand out by submitting two cartoons, one above the other—two for the price of one. At the same time, he had drawn a few strips in a new minimalist style. In 1949, he received an invitation from United Feature Syndicate to visit the head office in New York—and he took along the new minimalist strips. It turned out they wanted a four-panel strip, with some developed characters. At first, they asked Schulz to do separate panels of kids at the top and a strip of teenagers at the bottom. However, in the end, the little kids won out.

SAVING SPACE

In order to help sell the strip, the syndicate decided to reduce the strip in size and present it as a "space-saver." Comic strips at the time were typically about 7 ½ inches (19 cm) wide, running across four columns of newsprint. Schulz's strip would run across three columns, losing 2 inches (5 cm) in width. The small, nearly square panels were designed for maximum flexibility—they could be run horizontally, vertically, or stacked two by two. Schulz turned the small size into an advantage. He focused on paring down his strip to the simplest of lines and the

▲ The first strip featured an oval-headed Charlie Brown being coolly—even cruelly—appraised by his friends. From the start, Schulz intended his children's strip to have adult appeal.

briefest of incidents, with plenty of white space, in order to stand out on otherwise busy, crowded pages. This gave his strip a distinct look.

CHOOSING A NAME

Initially, the strip was to be named *Li'l Folk*, but to avoid a conflict with a similarly titled strip, Schulz agreed to a change in name. His suggestion was simple: *Charlie Brown* or *Good Ol' Charlie Brown*. However, the syndicate came up with its own suggestion: *Peanuts*. The name was intended to suggest small children, though to Schulz it suggested only "little insignificant things—things of little value." He also worried that readers would wonder who "Peanuts" was.

DEBUT

The first *Peanuts* strip appeared on the morning of October 2, 1950. It ran in seven newspapers nation-wide. Schulz had a five-year contract, with the syndicate owning the copyright on the characters and 50 percent of the profits. For the first month of strips, which consisted of six strips a week, appearing Monday to Saturday, Schulz was paid $90. He had arrived!

▶ Billed as the "greatest little sensation since Tom Thumb," *Peanuts* was advertised in newspapers in the hope that readers would write in to request it.

The Anatomy of *Peanuts*

The characters in *Peanuts* have a unique anatomy that helped them to stand out on crowded newspaper pages. In 1950, most child characters in comic strips, such as Hank Ketcham's *Dennis the Menace*, were three heads tall with relatively normal proportions. Schulz's characters were just two heads tall, with heads that were about the same height as the rest of their bodies. Despite his remarkably consistent penwork and art style, changes did take place over the years.

"Every cartoonist refines and changes his characters as he goes along," said Schulz in 1975.

SUBTLE CHANGES

In the earliest days, Charlie Brown's head is more oval than it would be later. He also has longer legs and a thinner torso. Snoopy is very much a puppy who walks on four legs. By the mid-1950s, Charlie Brown's head has become rounder and larger, and his torso is widened and elongated, while his legs have become shorter, and his feet are wide and flat. Snoopy begins to stand on two legs, with his ears hanging down. In the 1970s, Snoopy and Charlie Brown are at their most characteristic, with heads much larger in proportion to the rest of their bodies. In the 1980s, Schulz's drawing hand began to shake, and he had to learn to draw slowly with one hand supporting the other. The 1990s sees sketchier, looser versions of the characters, almost as if the characters have aged along with their creator.

1950s
Snoopy stands on all fours, with big, round ears and a pointed nose. Charlie Brown has an oval-shaped head and his torso, arms, and legs are relatively long and slender.

1960s
Snoopy stands on larger hind feet, with humanlike arms, and has a rounded snout with a black nose tip. Charlie Brown's body has filled out, and his head is now round.

1970s

The heads of both characters now dominate their bodies. Snoopy's ears flip up expressively when he is dancing.

1980s

Snoopy's belly has filled out and is especially prominent when lying on his doghouse (or sitting on Charlie Brown). His feet have grown nearly as large as Charlie Brown's. Schulz's penwork is more delicate as his drawing hand starts to shake with age.

1990s

The slightly jagged outlines of characters, a result of the shakiness of Schulz's hand in his later years, give them a delicate poignancy in the last decade of the strip.

This sign translates as "smiling is the done thing here" ("*ici le sourire est de rigueur*").

The painting of zebras is by Walter J. Wilwerding, an old friend and noted wildlife artist from Art Instruction Inc., the Minnesota art school where Schulz once taught.

NERVE CENTER

Charles Schulz's working area from his office in Santa Rosa, California, has been re-created in the Charles M. Schulz Museum, also in Santa Rosa. The exhibit features the tools of his trade within easy reach of his desk chair. Behind the desk and drawing board hang photos of his family, and all around are memorabilia, gifts, and books.

Schulz's original pens and nibs are on display here.

The surface of the desk and wall paneling behind are worn through with decades of use.

This is the drawing board that Schulz used from 1971–2000.

Working Methods

FAVORED PENS
Schulz's preferred pen for drawing was a Radio Pen No. 914, designed for writing, not drawing. When the original manufacturer Esterbrook & Co. went out of business in 1971, Schulz purchased the entire remaining stock of this nib. For speech balloons, he used a brand of calligraphy pen made by US manufacturer Speedball.

I n 1946, when he was 23 years old, Charles Schulz bought a professional drawing board with his first paycheck from his work as an art instructor. It cost $24 and it is thought he used it for the rest of his working life. At first, Schulz set up the drawing board in a room in his parents' house. Over the decades, he worked in a succession of studios. Each day, Schulz would sit at his drawing board and dream up *Peanuts* strips. He often began by doodling in pencil on a piece of paper. Schulz said, "I sit there and make up little conversations with myself,

thinking about the past, drawing Snoopy and the others in different poses, hoping something new will come along." Once the idea crystallized, he would sketch out the full strip in pencil then bring it to life with ink, breaking from his absolute concentration only for lunch or when his children came to see him after school. He also did his correspondence at his desk. Every week, he received hundreds of letters, which, at first, he would answer personally, often enclosing a drawing. Later, he dictated replies to his secretary. Schulz's desk was truly the center of his working life.

LETTERING EFFECTS
Different nibs allowed different effects, from the small, tight lettering of the early strips, to a heavier nib for Lucy's "loud shouting," and a heavier-still nib for Linus's "maximum screams!"

A CARTOONIST'S STUDIO
In the 1960s, Schulz worked in a purpose-built studio at his house in Sebastopol, California. In earlier days, he had worked at a desk improvised from a card table.

Original Artwork

Peanuts was initially designed to be a "space-saver," with four square panels that could be laid out horizontally, vertically, or in a block, depending on how the newspaper editor wanted to fill space on the page. For 38 years,

with a few variations, it remained this way. In January 1952, Schulz launched a longer strip on Sundays, which allowed him to develop more complicated story lines and have a greater variety of panel sizes. In February 1988,

the daily strip ended its strict four-frame format. Now Schulz had more flexibility to use the space in a variety of layouts, with as many as seven panels (but most often three) and sometimes just one.

FOUR-PANEL STRIP

Schulz used his four panels to pioneer a minimalist style that didn't depend on exaggerated characters or dramatic action. He became a master at handling empty space, simple setups, responses, and punch lines, and skillful use of pauses and occasional surreality.

"Once I have thought of an idea, I can visualize the entire page."
—Charles M. Schulz

SUNDAY STRIP

Knowing the reader's tendency to skip to the punch line, Schulz began to draw evermore eye-catching, stand-alone opening panels for the Sunday strips to attract attention.

LATER FORMAT

Schulz's later strips, from the 1980s onward, make effective use of the freedom to split the area in a variety of ways and utilize screentone dots to add shading to areas that would otherwise require handwork.

"I knew that little kids live a life that is different to the adults. It's tough to be a little kid."

—Charles M. Schulz

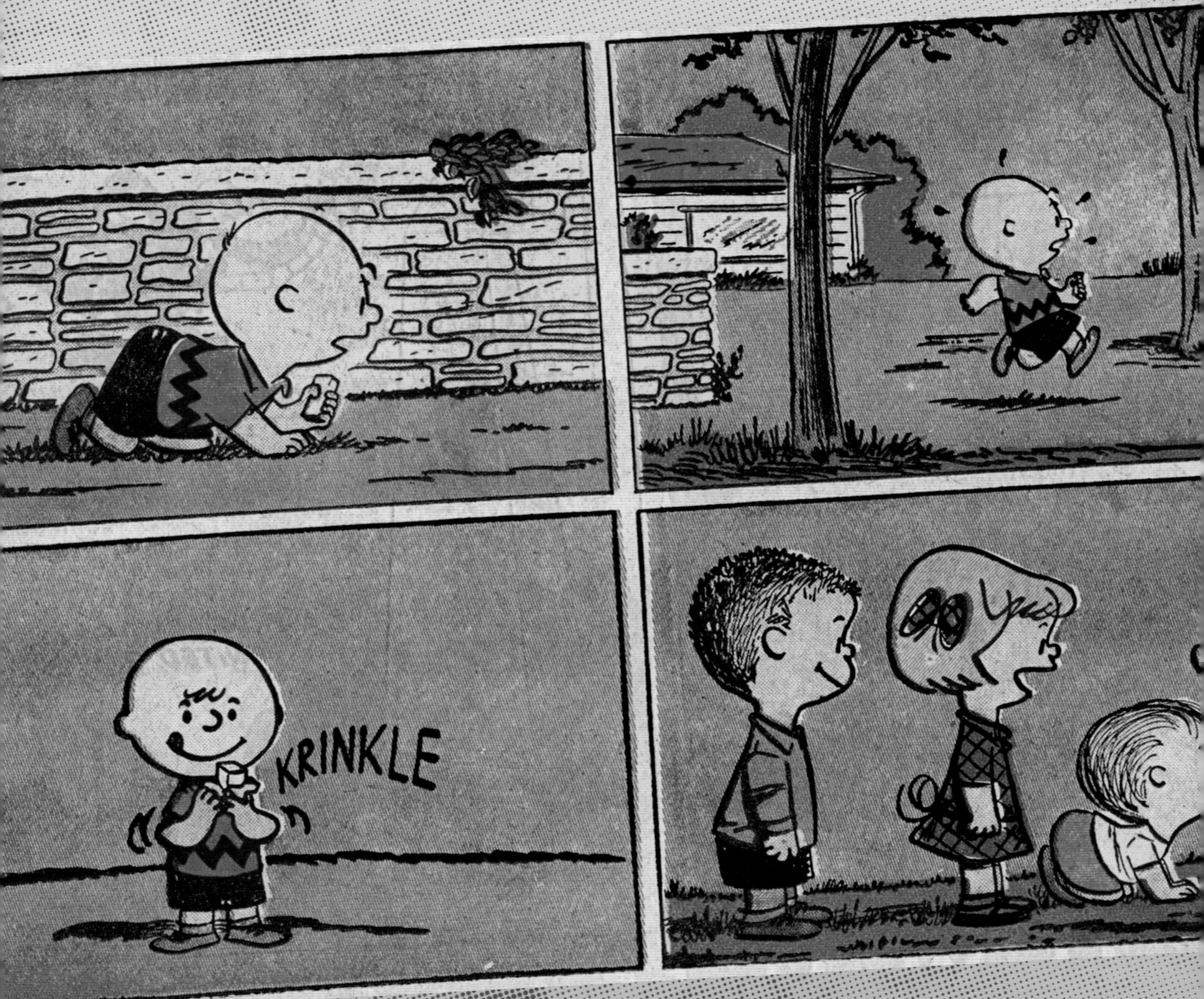
KRINKLE

The Originals

SCHULZ
!

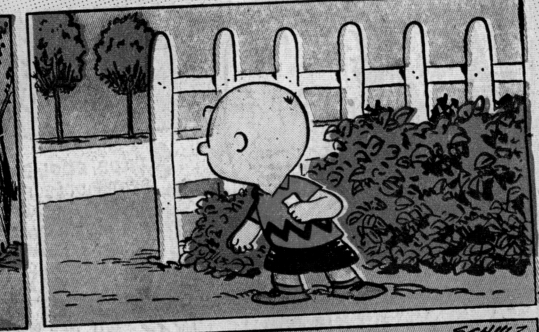

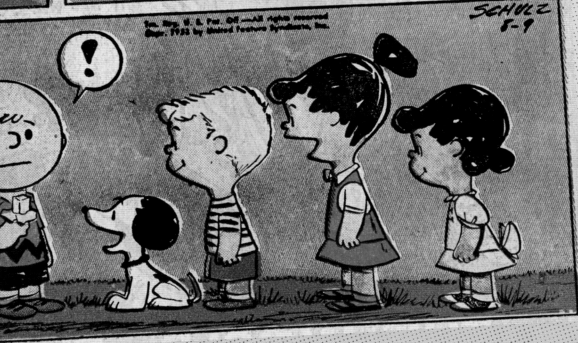

CHANGING SEASONS

This strip, from December 12, 1954, shows many
of the classic elements: low-rise suburban houses,
cultivated trees, neat yard fences—and snow!

The Setting

Where is *Peanuts* set? Schulz said, "I don't know where the *Peanuts* kids live. I think that, originally, I thought of them as living in these little veterans' developments, where Joyce [his first wife] and I first lived when we got married out in Colorado Springs." In June 1951, the Schulzes had moved from Minneapolis to Colorado Springs, which is at the eastern edge of the southern Rocky Mountains. Their home was a newly constructed, four-room cottage, bought with a veteran's loan. Despite a further move west to California in 1958 (after a return to Minneapolis), Schulz would always think of his strip as "very much Middle America." The kids live in the classic American suburban neighborhood, with tree-lined streets; rows of tidy, middle-income houses; a few vacant lots; and a municipal baseball field for public use. The sidewalks are wide, with well-tended lawns and cultivated trees and foliage. The seasons are clearly defined—with plenty of deep, thick snow and frozen lakes in winter. Schulz may have become a Californian, but he never left behind his homeland.

REAL-LIFE NEIGHBORHOOD
Tree-lined sidewalks, single-family homes, and big Buicks—a typical American suburb circa 1980. Macalester Street in St. Paul, Minnesota, is the neighborhood of one of Schulz's childhood homes.

Good Ol' Charlie Brown!

Charlie Brown's round face is an icon of the lovable loser, instantly recognized around the world. But Charlie Brown is also a complex character—much like Schulz himself.

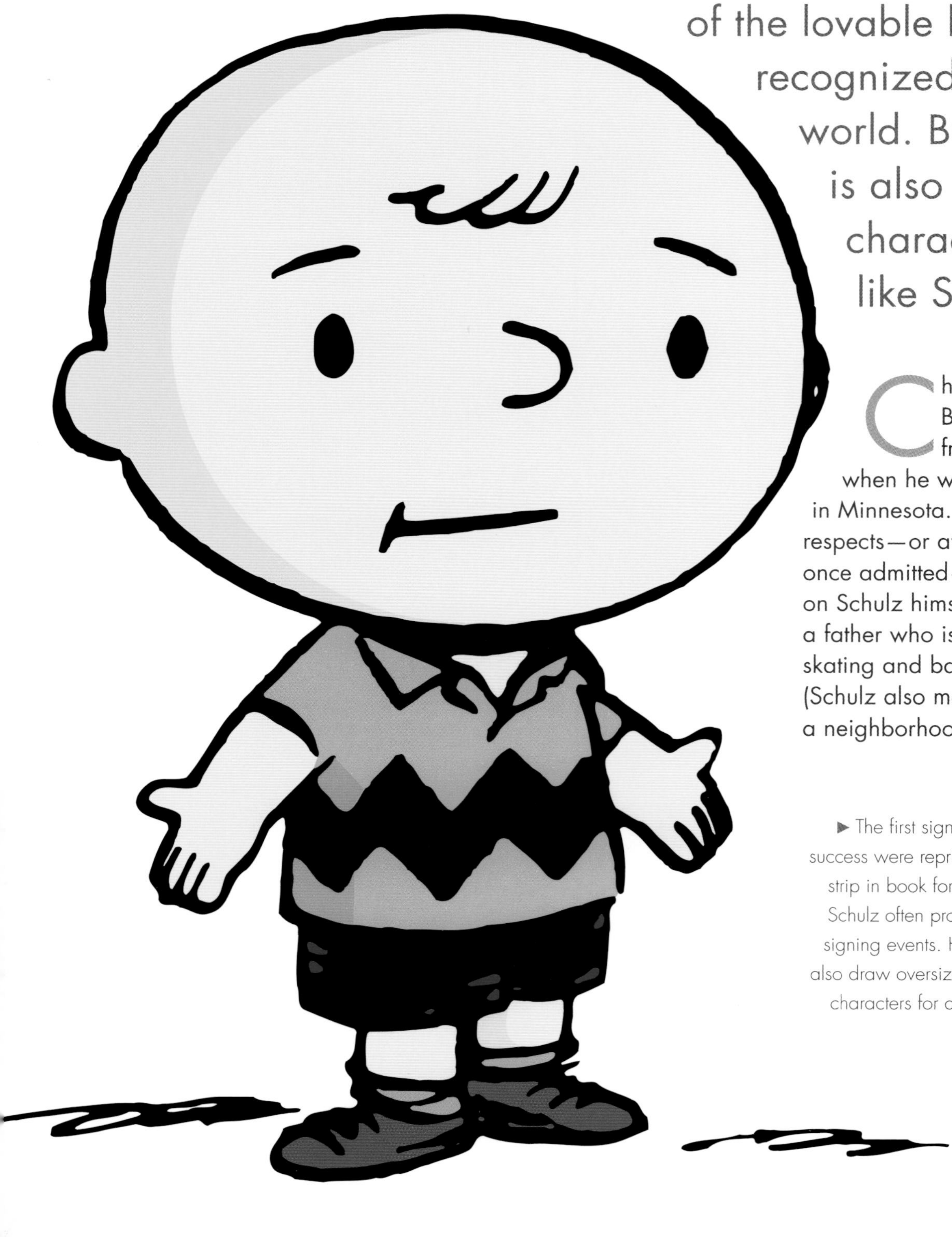

Charles Schulz gave Charlie Brown the same name as a friend and colleague of his when he worked at Art Instruction Inc., in Minnesota. However, in all other respects—or at least 60 percent, as he once admitted—Charlie Brown is modeled on Schulz himself. They share a biography: a father who is a barber, a love of ice-skating and baseball (Schulz also managed a neighborhood

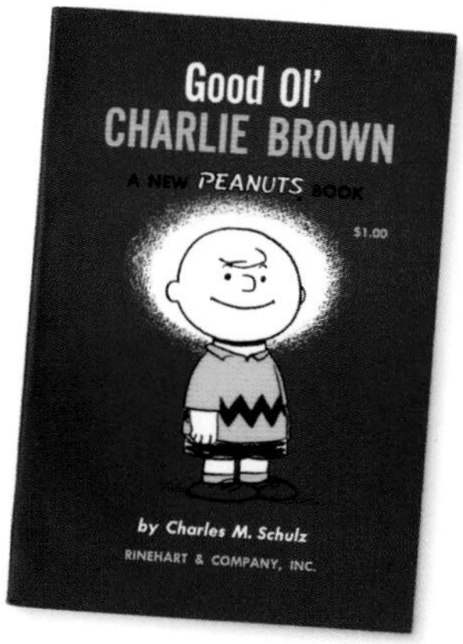
Good Ol'
CHARLIE BROWN
A NEW PEANUTS BOOK
$1.00
by Charles M. Schulz
RINEHART & COMPANY, INC.

► The first signs of early success were reprints of the strip in book form, which Schulz often promoted at signing events. He would also draw oversize *Peanuts* characters for attendees.

◄ The earliest Charlie Brown had a slightly oval face. As the 1950s progressed, Schulz began drawing his head larger and rounder.

▶ Internalized disappointment, disparities of social status—Schulz's strip brought a new seriousness to the "funnies" in 1950s America.

baseball team as a boy), and an obsession with a certain little red-haired girl. They shared similar insecurities and worries. But, as Schulz was at pains to explain, Charlie Brown is all of us: "People who win all the time are the minority; most of us lose."

SOCIAL UNCERTAINTY

In the very first *Peanuts* strip, on October 2, 1950, Charlie Brown's friend Shermy watches him strolling happily down the street. Shermy says, "Good ol' Charlie Brown …

▲ For the first few months of the strip, Charlie Brown wore a plain white shirt. Schulz introduced the now-famous zigzag-patterned shirt in December 1950, realizing it would help Charlie Brown stand out.

▶ Schulz never tired of drawing Charlie Brown's large, weightless head and wide range of expressions. Many artists have admired his skill at achieving just the right pen line to make the character work.

How I hate him!" Poor Charlie Brown. His friends like him, but they also resent him in some indefinable way. It's not for anything he does: Charlie Brown is unfailingly kind to his friends and loves his family. Even though, in these earliest strips, he has a spirited side, throwing an unprovoked insult at a friend then running away, shrieking gleefully, "I get my laughs!"

CRUEL CHILDHOOD

As time goes on, Charlie Brown becomes the mouthpiece of all the doubts, fears, and loneliness that we all feel (and not just as kids). He is, as often as not, mocked for it: Schulz knew that children can be cruel! Charlie Brown wants to be liked by everyone, and this, Schulz believed, makes him vulnerable.

Charlie Brown quickly learns to cope with disappointment. At one stage, everything he owns seems to be much smaller than that of his friends': his train track, his pumpkin, and his kiddie pool, which is just a tin bucket! Charlie Brown sees it, knows it, but says nothing, just a sigh or a resigned "good grief!" Our hearts go out to the round-headed kid.

STRENGTH OF CHARACTER

Charlie Brown expresses the insecurities that are part of the human condition. We love Charlie Brown all the more because he somehow keeps trying and stays smiling. And slowly, over the next few years, more and more readers are converted to seeing the world through Charlie Brown's eyes. Good ol' Charlie Brown!

Good Grief, Charlie Brown!

Charlie Brown has no luck—from failures at sporting events to battles with a kite-eating tree and insults from so-called friends. The worst thing is, they happen again and again. Schulz established most of these recurring incidents in the early years of the strip. For Charlie Brown, life is hard!

INSULTS

When Violet first calls Charlie Brown a "blockhead" in 1951, she unleashes an unending stream of abuse that only gets worse when Lucy enters the frame. He's called "wishy-washy" so many times, he starts to call himself that. (How wishy-washy can you get?)

FEEDING SNOOPY

Every day, Charlie Brown has to feed Snoopy. To ease the routine, he initiates twists—often sarcastic ones such as offering Snoopy a menu. Snoopy remains unimpressed, especially when his dinner is late!

BASEBALL

Charlie Brown loves sports, but sports do not love him. From as early as 1951, he plays baseball with his friends, emerging as team manager. However, success eludes his team in an infinite number of ways—and Charlie Brown suffers the repeated indignity of having his clothes knocked off by a fast-returning line drive.

PENCIL-PAL

In 1958, Charlie Brown begins writing to an overseas pen pal—although he makes such a mess using a pen that he reverts to a pencil, so his pen pal becomes a "pencil-pal." (Linus wonders if he could find himself a "crayon-pal" and Snoopy a "paw-print pal.") Much later, in the 1990s, it is revealed that his pencil-pal is a girl named Morag, and she lives in Scotland.

FOOTBALL

Almost every autumn at the start of the football season, Lucy holds the football for Charlie Brown to kick. Each time, she tricks him and moves the ball. In fact, it was Violet who kick-started this routine back in 1951.

KITE FAILING

Another certainty in Charlie Brown's life is that whenever he tries to fly a kite, it will manage to get the better of him. If it's not the kite that refuses to fly—sometimes even physically attacking him—it'll be the Kite-Eating Tree claiming another victim. In fact, Charlie Brown's first attempt to fly a kite, in 1952, is a qualified success—though the string is only just longer than his arms (he's afraid of airplanes).

UNHAPPY VALENTINE'S DAY

Here's how Charlie Brown typically spends Valentine's Day: sitting on the sidewalk next to his mailbox with a big smile on his face, confidently waiting for the mailman to bring him lots of valentines. By sundown, the smile has become a defeated frown. "Well, that's the way it goes."

The Original Trio

Before Schroeder, Lucy, and Linus, there was Shermy, Patty, and Violet. This original trio of friends dominate the early years of the strip.

▲ Patty demonstrates Schulz's view that the early strip "was based on the cruelty that exists among children."

Shermy is Charlie Brown's sole male friend at first. He's more confident than Charlie Brown. Where Charlie Brown tries and fails, Shermy excels—whether it's pumpkin carving, playing marbles, or sports. Despite claiming to "hate" Charlie Brown in the first strip, the two mostly get along fine. Shermy appears to be a little older than Charlie Brown, and they sometimes have "real adult conversations" as they stroll around the golf course or get hot dogs (Shermy in a dapper Hawaiian

"I only draw from my own experiences."
—Charles M. Schulz

WHAT SHALL WE PLAY ?

◄ The original gang in their distinctive styles: Shermy (before he got his trademark crew cut hairstyle), Violet with her ponytail, and Patty with her bob and checked dress. Snoopy is still a nonspeaking puppy.

▲ Shermy gets a crew cut, which becomes his style thereafter. Schulz has said he "disliked" drawing Shermy's hair.

▲ Whenever Patty and Violet exclude Charlie Brown, they expect to hurt his feelings. Sometimes, however, he gets the last laugh by simply telling them they're doing the right thing.

shirt). As the years go by, Shermy has fewer speaking appearances. After 1969, Shermy quietly disappears and is seen no more.

PATTY

Patty is the first—and for a time, only—girl in the strip. Like Shermy, she appears older than Charlie Brown and sometimes plays a protective role toward him. But she can be unthinkingly cruel: unprovoked, she thumps Charlie Brown while singing that little girls are made of sugar and spice. Patty introduces Charlie Brown to baby Schroeder, who lives next door, thus initiating a great friendship. Like Shermy, Patty's role becomes consigned to cameos only, especially after the introduction of the similarly named Peppermint Patty in 1966.

VIOLET

Violet is the new girl in 1951. At first, she makes endless mud pies for Charlie Brown and even

has a small crush on him. But soon, she forms a girl gang with Patty (and, later, Lucy) and delights in tormenting Charlie Brown. She boasts that she is better off than Charlie Brown and attempts to socially exclude him by not inviting him to parties. Schulz remembered this happening in seventh grade— though not to him personally: "I knew I didn't have a ghost of a chance of being invited anyway."

INSPIRATIONS

Schulz liked to give his characters the names of people he knew. Shermy is named after his teenage best friend, Sherman Plepler, and Patty shares a name with Schulz's cousin, Patricia Swanson. He based Violet on a woman he dated, Judy Halverson, who turned down his offer of marriage. (He ended up marrying her sister, Joyce.) Ultimately, though, he recognized that "some characters just don't seem to have enough personality to carry out ideas."

▲ Violet bakes a special batch of mud pies sprinkled with coconut—which Charlie Brown hates. Schulz also hated coconut.

▲ Shermy in his Hawaiian shirt eating hot dogs with Charlie Brown.

Irrepressible Puppy

▲ Schulz's talented childhood dog, Spike, became the model for Snoopy.

Snoopy evolved from a cute puppy to a breakout star with a rich inner life.

As a child, Schulz's family had a dog called Spike, who recognized more than 50 words and ate small metal objects apparently without harm. Spike was immortalized in Schulz's first published drawing, when Schulz was 16 years old. When Schulz began *Peanuts*, he planned to introduce a little dog inspired by Spike, whom he wanted to call Sniffy. However, he discovered that the name was already in use for another cartoon dog. Then he remembered a name that his mother had suggested for another dog if they ever had one: Snoopy!

SNOOPY'S DEBUT

Snoopy made his debut in 1950 in the third-ever *Peanuts* strip. At this time, he was a little puppy, walking on all fours, without thoughts. He wasn't solely Charlie Brown's dog at first, appearing in various houses,

◄ Snoopy was "just kind of a cute little puppy" at first, according to Schulz. But making him walk on two legs and have thoughts was "probably one of the best things that I ever did."

▲ Snoopy impersonates Mickey Mouse's ears—which, though iconic, are rigid, unlike Snoopy's own constantly shifting, expressive ears.

▲ Charlie Brown "teaches" Snoopy to walk on two legs. Over the years, it is more and more common to see him standing like a human. Snoopy even forgets he's a dog sometimes!

wherever he could find food and shelter. He wasn't even a beagle: that wouldn't be established until the 1960s. In time, Snoopy began to do undoglike things, such as wearing glasses, putting on a zigzag shirt like Charlie Brown's, imitating other animals such as sharks and snakes, and by 1952, revealing his thoughts. He occasionally danced on two paws, and eventually Charlie Brown taught him to walk—or thought he did because Snoopy mastered it in an instant with absolutely no apparent effort. (Although somehow he had been able to skate on two legs before this— there's nothing predictable about Snoopy!)

EXPRESSIVE PERSONALITY

Once Snoopy begins to have thoughts, he starts to resent having to rely on humans. He imagines what his life would be like if he were a wolf or a vulture. At this stage, he is still shamefaced when anyone witnesses his antics, but he will come to unapologetically embrace a range of personas. He has begun to live by his own rules and act out his desires, no matter how weird or ridiculous. Snoopy is simply not burdened by neuroses like all the other characters are. He dances like a teenager, kisses like a child, and is always irredeemably himself. It is no wonder that, by the late 1950s, Snoopy was fast becoming an international star, with a burgeoning merchandise industry emerging around him.

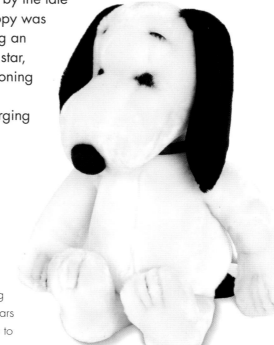

▶ The first Snoopy toys appeared in 1958, capturing his early look. However, it would take another 10 years for this first plush Snoopy toy to be manufactured due to a trademark dispute over the name "Snoopy."

Snoopy's Doghouse

Snoopy's home is no ordinary doghouse. It's anything he wants it to be!

At first, Snoopy lives in a regular doghouse situated in the backyard beside Charlie Brown's house. Seen mostly in three-quarter view, it has a peaked roof, a simple one-room interior, and Snoopy's name written above the entrance. Snoopy often sleeps in the archway. But all is not what it seems. For a start, he has a color TV and aerial. Snoopy's doghouse is full of surprises—it is bigger on the inside than the outside and is loaded with features: a recreation room with a pool table, a cedar closet, stairs and carpets, as well as a Van Gogh painting, a clock radio, books, records, and a photo of 1960s falsetto-voiced crooner Tiny Tim, among other curiosities.

UPPER TERRACE

In 1958, Snoopy begins sleeping on the top of his doghouse (or as he once called it, the "terrace"). This becomes Snoopy's primary place of residence, where he types his novels, meets with his bird friends,

◄ Schulz suggested that Snoopy may have used his ears to cling to the top of his doghouse, like birds instinctively clinging onto a branch with their feet.

◄ Poor Snoopy loses everything in the fire that burns his doghouse down—even his pinking shears! The tragedy means that even the World War I Flying Ace temporarily cannot fly his Sopwith Camel.

▲ Snoopy's doghouse has been destroyed a few times, the first being when Snoopy and Linus fight over possession of the security blanket.

and strafes the Red Baron (as the World War I Flying Ace). Schulz began to draw the doghouse more often side-on, so it functions as a stage for Snoopy's flights of fantasy. He recognized that Snoopy had become "a character so unlike a dog that he could no longer inhabit a real doghouse." Peppermint Patty once moved in, thinking it was Charlie Brown's guest cottage. Linus also moved in when Lucy threw him out of their house.

DEADLY THREATS

Sadly, Snoopy lost all his possessions when the doghouse burned down in a fire in 1966—which paralleled a fire in Schulz's own drawing studio earlier that same year, destroying many of his own treasured possessions. Snoopy gets a new doghouse (he and Charlie Brown work on the plans together), but he never gets back his Van Gogh: instead, he has an Andrew Wyeth, then one of Schulz's favorite American painters. Wyeth returned the compliment by sending Schulz a drawing of his own dog.

▲ The first time the full extent of the inside of Snoopy's doghouse is hinted at is when the gang all crawl in for a look.

► Snoopy's first attempts at sleeping on the roof of his doghouse resulted in a few tumbles. He soon gets the hang of it, but he occasionally rolls off when it's icy or if there's a strong wind.

Sincerely Schroeder

◄ Schulz's own daughter, Meredith, had a toy piano, inspiring him to introduce one into the strip for its then-newest, youngest member, Schroeder.

In *Peanuts*, Schroeder is the resident toy-piano-playing whiz kid, Beethoven fanatic, and all-round artistic genius.

Schroeder is a baby when we first meet him in May 1951. A few months later, he's grown into a little boy. Now wearing his trademark T-shirt with black stripes, Schroeder gets his first go on a toy piano, courtesy of Charlie Brown. Ta-da—instant virtuosity. From now on, Schroeder's life will revolve around music, with occasional breaks to play baseball and celebrate Beethoven's birthday. His love of Beethoven above all other classical composers started as a toddler, when Charlie Brown read him the life of Beethoven (which Schroeder preferred to fairy tales). Charlie Brown also gave him his first bust of Beethoven, which is often displayed on the end of his piano to inspire him. Schroeder is a virtuoso on the toy piano, despite the black keys just being painted on, but give him a real piano and he'll freeze up!

▶ When Schroeder is not playing piano or celebrating Beethoven's birthday, he plays on the neighborhood baseball team, as Charlie Brown's stalwart catcher.

◄ Schroeder with his piano and bust of Beethoven in a hand-carved music box made in 1968 by Italian company ANRI.

▲ The moment when Schroeder first plays piano. The notes in Schroeder's music are actually notes from different piano scores, which Schulz copied out very carefully.

SCHROEDER AND LUCY

In January 1953, a momentous event occurs. Lucy sits at the end of Schroeder's piano and asks what he's playing. When he tells her it's the *Nutcracker Suite*, she is delighted: "He called me sweet!!" Infatuation is born, though sadly Schroeder does not reciprocate—Beethoven, after all, was a lifelong bachelor. Over the decades, Lucy tries every which way to get Schroeder's attention: she alternately flatters and mocks him for his love of music. Schroeder doesn't seem to mind her being on the end of his piano, and he often uses the opportunity to educate her about music, but when she starts to imagine their married life he gets annoyed.

REAL-WORLD INSPIRATION

Schroeder's name was inspired by a boy that Schulz used to caddy with at a golf course in his hometown of St. Paul, Minnesota. Schulz toyed with making his own favorite

composer, Brahms, the favorite of Schroeder, too. But Brahms lost out to Beethoven, as Schulz thought that the way Beethoven sounded and looked on the page was funnier. Over many years of the strip, Schroeder celebrated Beethoven's birthday—and so did Schulz in the 1960s, hosting a party at his home in California where he drew Beethoven sweatshirts for the guests!

▲ Schroeder celebrates Beethoven's birthday on December 16 each year. Lucy often joins in, in a vain attempt to win Schroeder's affection.

▶ Snoopy is a fan of Schroeder's playing. He often gets carried away and jumps up on the piano to dance.

▶ Flattery is just one of the ways in which Lucy attempts to get Schroeder to love her back. She also tries to engage him about Beethoven, despite not really knowing anything about him, and seeing him chiefly as her love rival.

▲ Charlie Brown is drawn to the consoling comforts of a sad tune in this strip from 1953. Schulz was a fan of country music, with its songs of heartbreak and loss.

Proud of My Record Collection

The story of our lives always has some kind of soundtrack, and *Peanuts* is no different.

Peanuts and music are inextricably linked, from Schroeder at his toy piano to the distinctive jazz soundtracks that Vince Guaraldi gave to the TV specials. Schulz was a great fan of music—though he had to be persuaded on Guaraldi as jazz wasn't then to his taste. At the end of the war, he became a serious collector of classical records. He and his friends at Art Instruction Inc. even had an after-hours records appreciation club. They would whistle a theme from a symphony or concerto and see who could identify it. Schulz, like his father, was an expert whistler—a skill he gave to several characters, most notably Woodstock. His later tastes ran to a wide range of genres, especially country music.

Schulz spoke of how a particularly "depressing" Hank Williams song inspired him to introduce the Little Red-Haired Girl as Charlie Brown's lost love. He also named a short-lived cat character, Faron, after country singer Faron Young.

▶ Many early gags revolve around the gang listening to kids' tunes with the appreciation of connoisseurs. Here, Charlie Brown believes "The Sugar-Plum Tree" may be an acquired taste.

◀ A record player was a vital component of modern sitting rooms, the perfect accompaniment to the stylish postwar furniture, textiles, artworks, and lamps seen in the strips—even if the lyrics of songs were sometimes puzzlingly outdated!

> "[My dad] kept a record player across from his drawing table and a stack of LPs waiting to be heard."
>
> —Monte Schulz

▲ Jazz pianist Vince Guaraldi's 1965 soundtrack album features the *Peanuts* classic, "Linus and Lucy." For tracks featuring a children's choir, Guaraldi and producer Lee Mendelson chose less-than-perfect takes, wanting "kids to sound like kids."

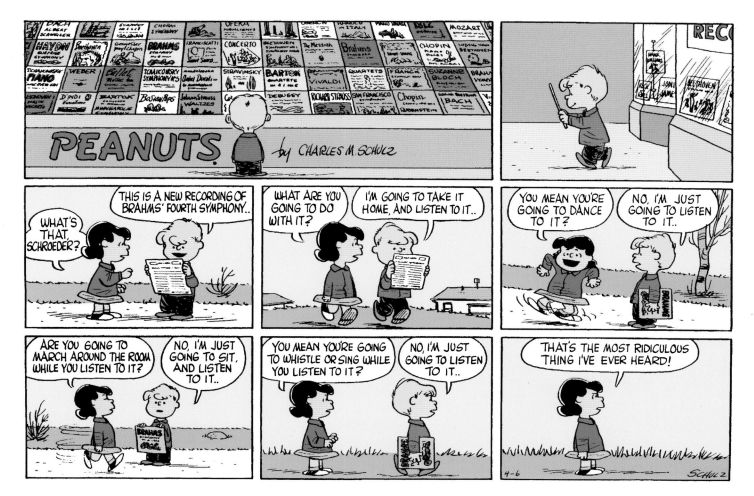

▲ Schroeder takes music very seriously indeed, much to Lucy's bemusement. Long-playing records (LPs) were a recent postwar invention, especially suited for longer classical works.

The Sunday Pages

I n January 1952, Schulz introduced the first Sunday strip. Typically presented in color, Schulz would draw the strip in black and white and select the colors using a chart, which the syndicate itself would then add in. With as many as 10 or 12 panels in these strips, Schulz often drew the final panel first, to ensure the punch line could be delivered effectively. He found that he sometimes thought of an idea that proved impractical to draw, and "it is far better to discover this by drawing the last panel first than after the entire page has been completed."

ADDING COLORS
Schulz colored photocopies of his Sunday strips by hand. He annotated them with numbers that corresponded to color charts held at the printer, where the final version was created.

FIRST SUNDAY
The whole gang has the space to play tag with Snoopy
in the first-ever Sunday strip on January 6, 1952.

The Head of the Household

Lucy is a big personality in a neighborhood that is almost too small to contain her.

When Lucy enters the strip in March 1952, she is just a baby who likes to make a fuss at bedtime. As she grows older, her fussing becomes her signature characteristic—something she refines and amplifies, and would never apologize for. Once Lucy finds her voice, the strip would never be the same again.

NO HOLDS BARRED

Lucy questions everything and everyone with a merciless (and often cruel) honesty. She is like a wrecking ball in the otherwise mild and introspective world of the strip, raging against Charlie Brown for being "wishy-washy" and reducing gentle Linus to a quivering wreck (no wonder he needs that security blanket). As Schulz said, "She can cut through a lot of the sham, and she can really feel what is wrong with Charlie Brown, which he can't see himself." Of course, she is frequently blind to her own faults and is often frighteningly

◀ Lucy is confident, self-assured, difficult, and sometimes cruel. There's no doubt in her mind, however, that she's "head of the household."

► In her first appearances, Lucy has "toddler" eyes. Despite being younger, she doesn't take long to figure out how to humiliate Charlie Brown.

ill-informed (and won't tolerate being corrected), but her single-mindedness never lets being wrong get in the way. If in doubt, yell!

BREAKING THE GLASS CEILING

Lucy's wish is to be free and uninhibited: she even warns Linus not to color in the lines because it leads to inhibition. Her expectations from life are huge: she doesn't want "ups and downs," she just wants "ups and ups and ups." She even wants a whole year to be dedicated to her (1969, if you're asking). Constantly searching for ways to utilize her

drive, intellect, and ambition, Lucy's ultimate goal is to be president, followed quickly by queen.

DESTRUCTIVE URGES

Life is not all "ups" for Lucy, however, and, like Charlie Brown, she is prone to depression. Unlike him, she doesn't mope; she expresses it in anger and frustration. As she says, "I feel torn between the desire to create and the desire to destroy." And while Charlie Brown irritates her to distraction (and vice versa), they can't seem to leave each other alone. No wonder Joyce, Schulz's

wife at the time, said, "Sparky is really Charlie Brown, and I guess I'm Lucy, though I don't like to admit it."

SINGLE WEAKNESS

Schulz also put some of himself into Schroeder, the introspective artist. And Schroeder is Lucy's weakness. She is locked into a seemingly endless battle to break through Schroeder's self-absorption and win his affection. Schroeder is the only character who can inspire thoughts of a quiet, domestic, married life in Lucy. As if!

▲ Lucy makes no apologies for her infatuation with Schroeder. Beginning in 1953, she sets herself the challenge of attempting to win his love, or, failing that, his attention.

▲ Lucy proves that she's almost more terrifying when she doesn't shout!

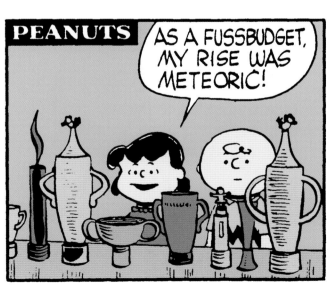

◄ Lucy is proud of her awards and achievements as a fussbudget. She tells Charlie Brown that one newspaper editor wrote, "This girl was born to fuss!"

► Snoopy is the only other character in the strip who is as uninhibited as Lucy, and, in rare moments of unalloyed joy for Lucy, they often dance together.

Wise Beyond His Years

Bright but innocent, Linus Van Pelt is the "house intellectual," according to Schulz.

Linus Van Pelt enters the strip in September 1952 as Lucy's baby brother. He and Charlie Brown quickly become friends, united against Lucy, who treats each of them without mercy. Linus is thoughtful, philosophical, and wise beyond his years—but also naive and innocent, and, of course, dependent on a blanket and a thumb for security (he's a total wreck when separated from his blanket—blanket-hating grandmothers take note!).

VOICE OF REASON

A great reader, Linus often quotes from classic literature and the scriptures (as well as many other subjects, ranging from music to sports, the law, psychiatry, and life itself). Despite his intellect, Linus also has an eccentric personal faith of his own: the Great Pumpkin, a Santa-Claus-like being who brings gifts for children (despite all evidence to the contrary). Charlie Brown supports Linus in this belief, as well as in his need to carry his security blanket around and suck his thumb, which others mock. Linus, in turn, generally supports Charlie Brown and, being thoughtful, understands and tolerates

► Schulz said that Linus came from a drawing he did one day of a face with "wild hair," which he thought was funny so he decided to put him in the strip. Schulz modeled Linus's blanket on his kids' own.

his need to complain. Elbow to elbow, they lean on a wall and share their worries. Linus is a rare voice of reason in the neighborhood and gets along with most people, including Snoopy—despite Snoopy always trying to steal Linus's blanket (and steal the glasses Linus wears for a short while).

UNASHAMED ECCENTRIC

Among Linus's eccentricities is talking to leaves and his fondness for patting birds on the head, which infuriates Lucy because she worries her family will become a laughingstock if word gets out. Linus can't understand what's wrong with it: "It makes the birds happy, and it makes me happy …"

FAVORITE CHARACTER

Schulz was a big fan of Linus. Named for a colleague of his at Art Instruction Inc., Linus Maurer, he liked how the "L" in Linus's name matched Lucy's name. Linus was also Schulz's favorite character to draw, and he liked how the character "can be very smart; he can be dumb; he can be innocent; he can be all-knowing; he can have the blanket and be completely dependent on it, but then again, you can take it away from him."

▲ "They come depressed, and they go away feeling great." So, what's wrong with patting birds on the head? Simple, according to Charlie Brown: "No one else does it." It also embarrasses Lucy. It's hard being an eccentric.

▲ Linus and Charlie Brown often rest their elbows on a wall in the neighborhood and share their hopes, dreams, and fears. Linus is a good listener and shows support for his beleaguered friend.

▲ Linus's inexplicable talents arrive early, as when he shows up Charlie Brown's pathetic efforts at building a house of cards. He also blows square balloons and sculpts life-size snowmen.

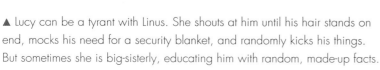

▲ Lucy can be a tyrant with Linus. She shouts at him until his hair stands on end, mocks his need for a security blanket, and randomly kicks his things. But sometimes she is big-sisterly, educating him with random, made-up facts.

Doin' His Own Thing

Cleanliness may be next to godliness, but for Pigpen it is next to impossible!

◄ For Pigpen, dirtiness is not a shameful thing, but an accomplishment. He certainly doesn't appreciate the rain for washing it away!

Pigpen enters the strip July 13, 1954, when Patty encounters him messing up an otherwise perfectly clean sandbox, though his favored environment is the mud puddle. Dressed in filthy overalls and with a dirt-smeared face, he wears his outsider status as a badge of honor. Having been called insulting names so often, he's just dropped his real name and adopted the most commonly used insult: Pigpen. Lucy says "Welcome to the gang" the instant she meets him. She knows a fellow misfit when she sees one.

DIRTY HABITS
Pigpen is completely comfortable living inside his own personal dust cloud. He doesn't go out of his way to get dirty; he just doesn't go out of

THEY DIDN'T RECOGNIZE ME!

7-23   SCHULZ

▲ Pigpen makes an occasional appearance all neat and tidy in order to go to a birthday party. Unfortunately, he isn't let in, as no one recognizes him.

▲ For Pigpen, a wash is a wipe around his eyes just so he can see where he's going.

▶ The gang meet Pigpen for the first time. As he says in his own defense, he may be dirty but at least he's consistent (and he's got clean thoughts).

▲ Snoopy gets caught in a passing dust storm.

his way to stay clean. He can scrub up if the need arises—and once did in an attempt to impress Patty. But even with spotless overalls, scrubbed face and hands, and hair combed neatly back, it only takes a walk along a street for the old Pigpen to return, as if by magic. He's past the point of no return! All the more reason to just be dirty and proud of it. He's just doin' his own thing!

UNLIKELY ROLE MODEL

The gang frequently suggests that Pigpen try to be neat. But mostly they accept him as he is; they even go through a short phase of imitating him (Snoopy included). Freedom can be liberating—perhaps that's why Pigpen was popular in the let-it-all-hang-out 1960s. He even inspired the nickname of the Grateful Dead keyboard player Ron "Pigpen" McKernan, who apparently had his own less-than-spotless habits. Despite the character's popularity, Schulz came to find Pigpen somewhat of a burden and his appearances became less frequent over the decades.

▲ Pigpen explains to Charlie Brown that "the dirt and dust of countless ages" are affixed to him. Charlie Brown later defends Pigpen as "carrying the dirt and dust of some past civilization." Dirtiness has nobility!

The Entitled Innocent

Sally Brown is not trying to fix the world. She has a hard enough time understanding it.

When the news is broken to Charlie Brown that he's going to be a brother, he couldn't be more excited and proud, handing out chocolate cigars to all his friends and buying footie pajamas for his little sister (with a zigzag pattern, of course). But he soon learns it's hard to be a role model. After all, Sally has the idea that a big brother should be strong and make you feel secure. Also, they shouldn't have a better bedroom than you (so she tries to steal it at every opportunity). Sally finds other role models. She bonds with Snoopy, who recognizes a fellow four-footer when she's at the crawling stage. They form a tag team to steal Linus's blanket, Sally distracting him with a kiss, while Snoopy lifts the blanket. Linus then tries to get Sally hooked on security blankets herself (she prefers beanbags!) and, later, initiates her into the mysteries of the Great Pumpkin. Sally rewards Linus by falling in love with him, calling him her "sweet babboo"—a term of endearment that Schulz's wife Jean used for Schulz. Linus doesn't return her affection, and often shouts at her, "I'm not your sweet babboo!" (even though, at the very beginning, it was Linus who had a short-lived crush on Sally).

SCHOOL DAZE

Life gets harder for Sally when she starts school. Despite being good-hearted, sweet, funny, and friendly, she just doesn't do well with formal education, as it requires that

▲ Sally is a complex, mixed-up individual. She likes to slide by doing as little work as possible. In fact, she'd like to just skip school and go straight to being a big TV star (or a hairdresser).

▶ While Charlie Brown singularly fails to protect his younger sister from teasing and bullies, he does frequently help her with her homework.

you memorize conjunctions, name rivers, and remember locker combinations. School exposes her lazy, naive side. Noticeably nonathletic, Sally would rather be sitting in her beanbag watching a good game show on television. Well, who wouldn't?

WHAT'S THE USE?
At school, Sally becomes known for malapropisms and misguided class reports on "Peter Rabbit and His Coat of Many Colors" and "Santa Claus and His Rain Gear." Explanations just further confuse her. Sally simply doesn't see the need to learn anything. For her, a term paper is something you dash off before breakfast on the day it should be handed in.

DEALING WITH IT
Sally, who is very sensitive, sees school as nothing but pressure and social programming. She starts opening her heart to the school building itself. This being *Peanuts*, the school responds and even falls a little bit in love with her—it likes the way she calls bricks "cool"—and becomes very protective of her. Sally finally finds a way of dealing with life—through her philosophies: first "Who cares?" then "Forget it," "All is well," and "We'll always have Minneapolis." Meaningless, sure, but from now on, nothing can touch her!

◀ Whenever Sally refers to Linus as her "sweet babboo," wherever he is, he hears and replies, "I'm not your sweet babboo." In 1991, she takes things a step further when she becomes his "babbooette."

▲ Sally is happiest in a beanbag watching TV. In fact, she once went to beanbag summer camp, where they did nothing but watch TV and eat junk food. She came back fat but signed up for another year anyway.

◀ Once, Sally was diagnosed with amblyopia (lazy eye), which had to be corrected with the use of an eye patch. Afterward, she gave the patch to Snoopy to wear as a pirate.

Good Ol' Charlotte Braun

Charlotte Braun is the only girl who has a built-in high-fidelity speaker (her voice!).

▲ Charlotte's voice is too much for poor Snoopy, who tries to wrap his own ears together to block out the sound.

ntroduced in November 1954, Charlotte Braun is the opposite of Charlie Brown: she's confident, outspoken, and TALKS VERY LOUDLY! And that's just her normal tone of voice. She can go louder—and higher. Yikes! Her ear-shattering tone reduces Charlie Brown to a quivering wreck. Linus is forced to retreat under his blanket. Even the girl gang refuses to play with her.

CHARACTER FLAW

Charlotte Braun is an early example of Schulz experimenting with new characters, but finding that some just don't have what it takes to make them stick. During her short-lived time in the strip, the high-volume gag runs dry, and Charlotte is no longer seen after February 1955. When librarian (and *Peanuts* fan) Elizabeth Swaim wrote to Schulz to ask him to drop the character from the strip, Schulz replied: "I am taking your suggestion."

◀ Charlotte Braun's appearances in the strip only just reach double figures (a total of 10).

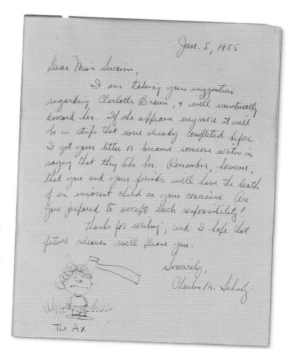

▶ In his reply, Schulz teased Swaim that she would "have the death of an innocent child" on her conscience—and pictured Charlotte Braun with an ax sticking out of her head!

This Tree Eats Kites

For Charlie Brown, flying a kite is an emotional experience.

► Charlie Brown warns Lucy about the dangers of the Kite-Eating Tree.

Over the years, kites have not only refused to fly, they have attacked him, flown down the sewer, and even exploded. But mostly they get chomped by the Kite-Eating Tree, sometimes with Charlie Brown dangling upside down wrapped in the string. The tree has a big grin and even makes chomping noises when it's eating. Schulz said, "When a kite becomes caught in a tall tree, it irretrievably and gradually disappears over a period of several weeks. So it seemed to me that the tree must be eating it."

Charlie Brown often talks to the tree, sometimes taunting it, sometimes even feeding it a kite in case it suffers from hunger. But he never gives up. Which is why Charlie Brown isn't a loser. For Schulz, "A real loser would stop trying."

▲ Lucy throws Schroeder's piano up into the Kite-Eating Tree because he refuses to pay attention to her. The tree appears to enjoy a change from its diet of kites, saying, "Chomp! Chomp! Chomp!"

► The Kite-Eating Tree chews up another one of Charlie Brown's delicious kites.

Sometimes Charlie Brown's baseball team resembles a theological seminary more than a ball club. Charlie Brown should never have asked why they needed to suffer defeats like they do.

The Losingest Team (in the History of Baseball)

The neighborhood baseball team is spectacularly unsuccessful. Well, it *is* managed by Charlie Brown!

Come rain or shine, Charlie Brown turns up for every game. But every game, his team loses. It's when he doesn't show up that they make an occasional win! Charlie Brown is pitcher as well as manager. His pitching is bad, resulting in line drives that knock him clean off the mound. His catcher, Schroeder,

can't throw and masks this by finding something he needs to say to Charlie Brown so that he can walk up to him and hand him the ball. Plus, he's paranoid about damaging his piano-playing fingers. The right fielder is Lucy, who always misses the catch because something gets in her eye: the sun, vapor trails, dandelions,

the future, hope ... though she can hit a home run if it includes the promise of a kiss from Schroeder. Snoopy, as shortstop, spends most games asleep (though he can catch with his mouth well enough). Linus tends to play second base, only his shoelaces are usually tied together. Anyway, official team statistician is more his scene: statistics about how

Charlie Brown explains to Linus which league they are in. Schulz said that his own childhood ball team lost a game 40 to 0, which is where he got the idea for Charlie Brown's string of losses.

IT'S GOING TO CLEAR UP....

◄ With Charlie Brown, there's little difference between determination, stubbornness, and stupidity.

many games they've lost don't lie (though, according to Charlie Brown, they do shoot off their mouth a lot). Pigpen either blends in with the dirt on the base he's covering or knocks up such a dust cloud that he can't see to run. Often, the gang gets wrapped up in a discussion about ethics or theology, forgetting to play completely. Although this reliably ineffective baseball team is famous for losing, they have won a few games over the years, mostly when Charlie Brown has nothing to do with it, either through sickness, injury, or being at camp.

CHILDHOOD INSPIRATION

Charles Schulz thought that baseball was the ideal sport for *Peanuts*. He liked its contemplative quality and its sense of suspense, which worked perfectly for the humor he used in the strip. As a teenager, he organized his very own version of Charlie Brown's baseball team, with the kids in his neighborhood. The team was named, for reasons unknown, the "Tetie Whops." Even though he was spending a lot of his spare time practicing his drawing, he always found time to play ball— just like Charlie Brown.

▲ What the gang lacks in baseball skills, they more than make up for in verbal dexterity.

◄ Always the sucker, Charlie Brown forgets that an offer of help from Lucy can only mask a hidden hate-bomb.

First Merchandise

Merchandising *Peanuts* began in the 1950s. The earliest items were reprints of the strip in paperback book form, published from 1952 by Rinehart & Company (later Holt, Rinehart and Winston). In 1957, Dell began to publish original comic books. However, this set of dolls, created by the Hungerford Plastics Corporation in 1958, took Schulz's characters off the page and into a three-dimensional medium for the first time. Re-creating the gang in their early, original appearances, the 6-inch- (15-cm-) tall figurines were molded from a then-new material, polyvinyl. The larger line of 9-inch- (23-cm-) tall dolls, shown here, was issued in 1961, with Charlie Brown's new baby sister, Sally, added to the range.

Like all the dolls, Charlie Brown (wearing a red shirt) issues a whistle noise when squeezed.

Snoopy was marketed simply as "Peanuts Dog."

An unusually clean-looking Pigpen is wearing his trademark overalls.

THE HUNGERFORD GANG
Each doll came packed in a clear plastic bag with a "hanger tag" featuring a comic strip. They were marketed as being made of "Safe, Sanitary, Unbreakable Vinyl."

Lucy was marketed under the name "Fuss Budget." As in the strip, she and Linus (and, later, Rerun) are the only characters with little lines at the sides of their eyes (giving them an out-of-focus look, according to Schulz).

The Linus doll originally would have carried a security blanket made of cloth over his shoulder.

Schroeder, with his piano and bust of Beethoven, is now the rarest doll.

Sally Brown appears in her earliest incarnation as a toddler.

Comics and More

Peanuts appeared in anthologies, spin-off comics, and new interpretations, as well as Schulz's other strips.

Since 1952, Schulz's original *Peanuts* strips have been reprinted in book form, first by Rinehart & Company (which then became Holt, Rinehart and Winston) and then by other publishers, beginning in the United States and soon around the world. These books featured selections of strips, but the entire 50-year run has now been published in full by the US publisher Fantagraphics. The ambitious project was first discussed with Schulz in 1997 and progressed after Schulz's death through the support of his widow, Jean Schulz. Many strips had not been reprinted since their original appearance in newspapers. Some proved incredibly difficult to track down, since the handful of newspapers that printed the strips in the earliest days no longer retain archival copies.

SCHULZ AND SASSEVILLE
Outside the newspaper strip itself, Schulz had a hand in many of the *Peanuts* comic books published by Dell, though he called in help from old friends from his Art Instruction Inc. days, including Jim Sasseville and Dale Hale, among others. While the original strips inside these comic books were mainly drawn by these cartoonists, Schulz occasionally drew interior stories and created the covers. Sasseville also drew many of the panels for a separate newspaper

It's Only a Game ran for just over a year, from November 1957 to January 1959. Schulz often drew the pencil sketches, while Sasseville (uncredited) did the inking and lettering.

▶ The Seattle-based publisher Fantagraphics issued, over 12 years at a rate of two volumes per year, the entire 50-year run of *Peanuts* strips in hardback volumes designed by Canadian cartoonist Seth.

strip that Schulz had begun in the late 1950s, *It's Only a Game*, which satirized the competitiveness of people who played social games like bridge and golf.

> ## "Charles M. Schulz was the greatest comic strip artist ever."
> —Jim Sasseville

▲ In 1974, Charles Schulz made his one-and-only appearance at San Diego Comic-Con. He discussed his own days of being a comic book fan, drew sketches of *Peanuts* characters (and also Popeye!), and was joined onstage by *Peanuts* animation director Bill Melendez.

▲ These pages from Dell's *Nancy* comic, published in September and November 1957, feature original—though unsigned—art by Schulz himself.

▲ Inspired by Dell Comics' classic strips, California-based publisher BOOM! Studios began producing original *Peanuts* comic books in 2011.

"You have to put yourself, all of your thoughts, all of your observations, and everything you know into the strip."

—Charles M. Schulz

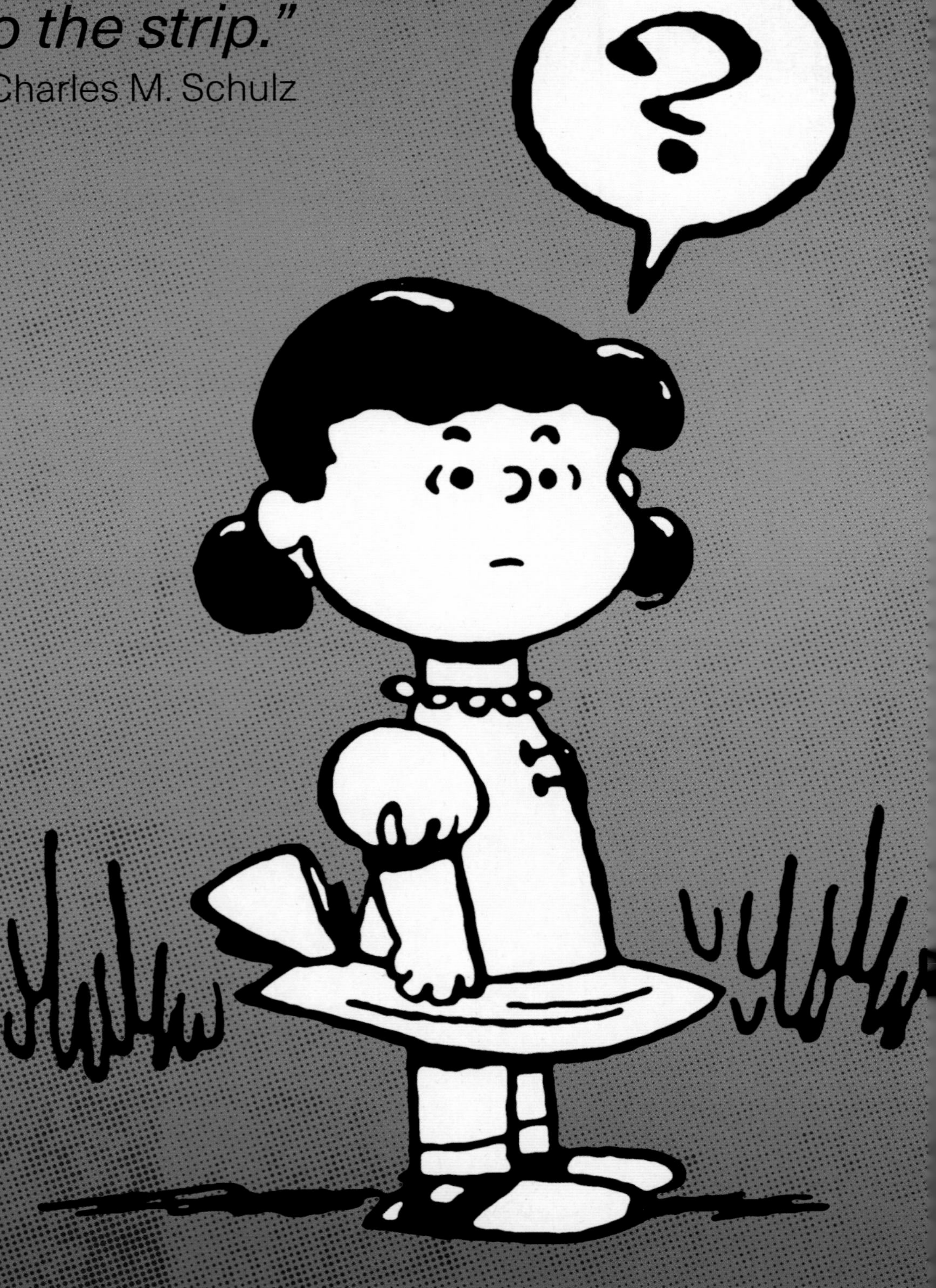
?

Going Global

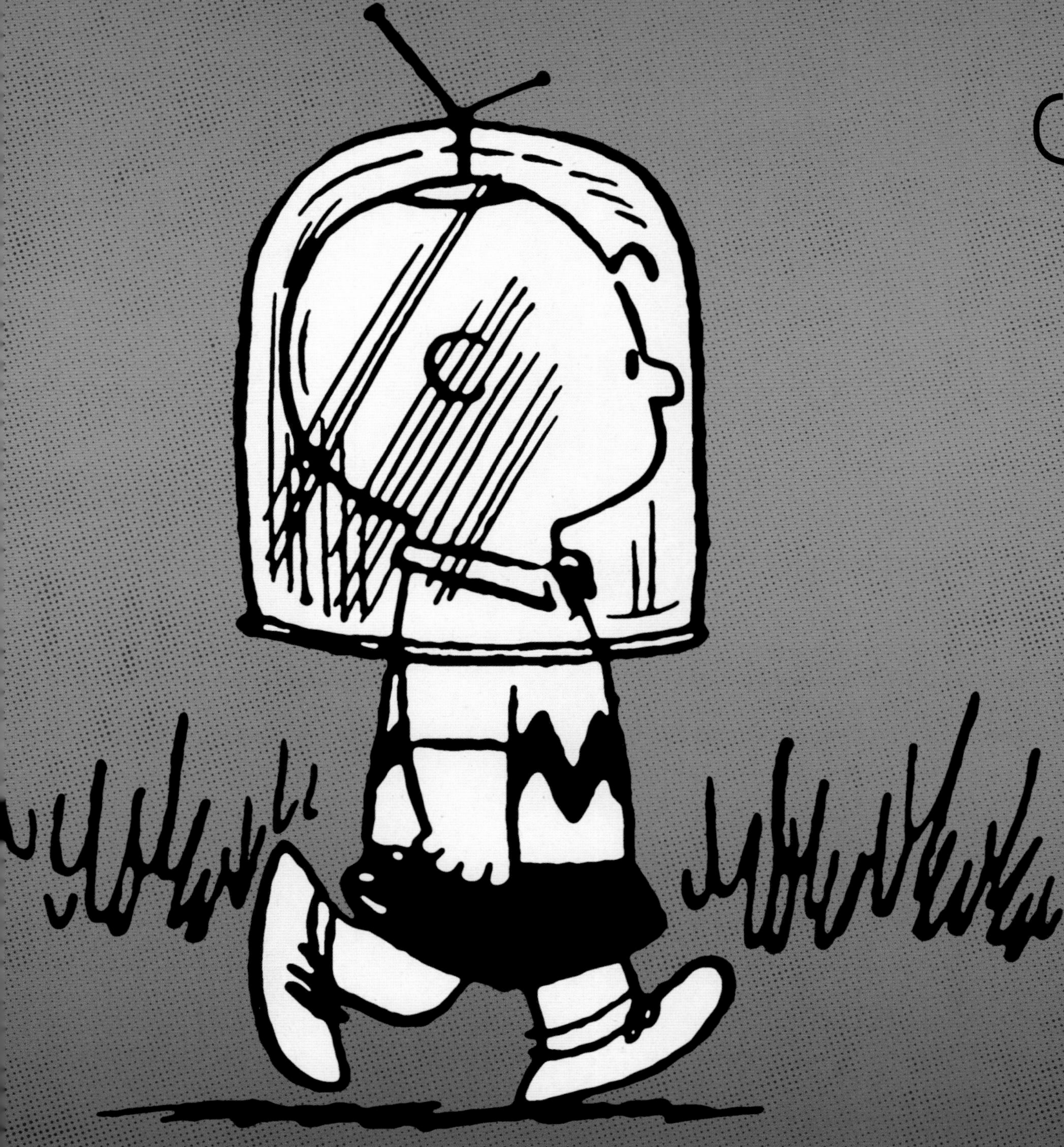

Universal Language

1

By the 1960s, critical mass had been reached, Schulz was at the height of his fame, and *Peanuts* went global, resulting in fun and unique translations across the world. With *Carlitos* ("Charlie Brown" in Spanish), *Replica* ("Rerun" in Italian), and *Snobben* ("Snoopy" in Swedish), the whole world was making Schulz's characters their own, through books, toys, homewares, and much more!

2

3

4

5

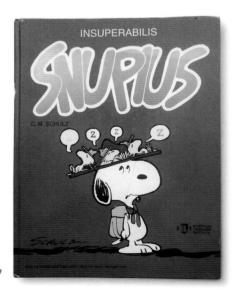

6

7

8

9

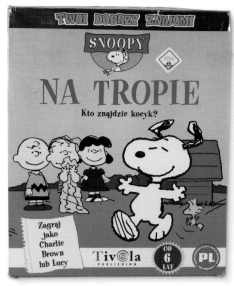

10

11

12

13

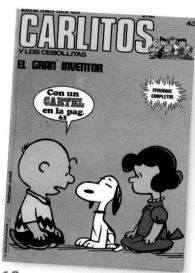

14

15

16

1 *Søndags Radiserne: Tegnet og fortalt af Charles M. Schulz*; Gyldendal (1988, Danish)   2 *Snobben och kärleken*, Känguru (2008, Swedish)
3 *Fiffigt, Snobben*; Wahlströms (1983, Swedish)   4 *Suku on rakkain, Ressu*, Sanoma Osakeyhtiö (1983, Finnish)   5 *Anong Say Mo, Snoopy?*
Felta Book Sales Company (1975, Filipino)   6 *Z. Z. Z. Snoopy*, Kadokawa Shoten (2019, Japanese)   7 *Insuperabilis Snupius*, European Language
Institute (1984, Latin)   8 *No Pots Guanyar, Charlie Brown!* Edicions 62 (1973, Catalan)   9 *Charlie Brown 'Cyclopedia, Volume 2, Animals Through
the Ages*; Science, Engineering & Education Co., LTD (1991, Thai)   10 *Na Tropie* (2002, Polish video game)   11 *Super Snoopy Book: Peanuts 35th
Anniversary, Special Edition*; Kadokawa Shoten (1985, Korean)   12 Happiness is a Warm Puppy, Twin Vision/American Brotherhood for the Blind
(1968)   13 *Láska podle Snoopyho: Vybrané stripy Peanuts z let 1966–1999* (2010, Czech)   14 *Ffyrnigrwydd Snwpi*, Gwasg y Dref Wen (1984, Welsh)
15 *Bonjour, Peanuts!*, Dupuis (France, 1968)   16 *Carlitos Y Los Cebollitas – El Gran Inventor*, Buru Lan, S. A. de Ediciones (1974, Spanish)

World Famous Snoopy

Snoopy is no plain ol' dog. Schulz said, "Snoopy refuses to be caught in the trap of doing ordinary things like chasing and retrieving sticks." Snoopy starts to impersonate animals like vultures, sharks, or wolves. "If I were a wolf, and I saw something I wanted, I could just take it," Snoopy reasons. (No more waiting for Charlie Brown to bring him his dinner.) Then he starts adopting whole personas, including author, attorney, hockey player, football star, swimmer, skier, surgeon, disco dancer, and grocery clerk—all "world famous," of course—always with more attitude than aptitude. Schulz said of Snoopy, "When I finally developed the formula of using his imagination to dream of being many heroic figures, the strip took on a completely new dimension."

FIERCE VULTURE
Snoopy thinks he would get more respect if he were a vulture. But Lucy stares him down, Linus tickles him, Violet tells him he has pretty eyes—and if no one's around, he gets lonesome.

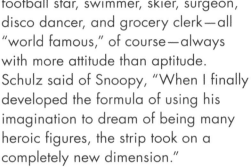

MASKED MARVEL
Who dares challenge Lucy, the arm-wrestling champion? Snoopy does, as the Masked Marvel. After a protracted wrestle, Snoopy breaks the deadlock ... by diving in with a kiss on Lucy's nose—an unfair move, according to her.

COWABUNGA!

In 1964, Snoopy's attempts to impress a cute beach beagle with his surfing skills ended in a wipeout. But by 1980, when this motorized toy was issued, he's become quite the surf dog!

"BEAU" SNOOPY

The World Famous French Foreign Legionnaire stands guard at Fort Zinderneuf on the edge of nowhere. He has joined this "legion of lost souls" to forget. He marches across the desert without water … until Sally brings him his water bowl.

WORLD FAMOUS AUTHOR

Snoopy composes his next, great work of literature, as seen in this original art layout from 1969. When Snoopy writes his autobiography, Linus comments, "Everything that happened to you only happened in your imagination."

WORLD FAMOUS ATTORNEY

When Peppermint Patty decides to fight her school over the dress code (she refuses to wear a dress), she calls her "world famous" attorney to help. Together they lose the case—but she still hires him several more times (as do others).

That Round-Headed Kid

To Snoopy, he's "that round-headed kid." To Charlie Brown, Snoopy is plain out of his mind. But they both need each other.

▲ One of the rituals in the strip is Charlie Brown feeding Snoopy. Snoopy's reaction is often joyous, sometimes sarcastic or caustic, but never predictable.

It can't be easy having a dog like Snoopy. But then Snoopy would say the same about having an owner like Charlie Brown. Their relationship is close, but complicated, and they both need different things from each other. Snoopy pretends that all he needs is dinner, and he doesn't appreciate it being even a minute late and certainly not with a side order of Charlie Brown's prankish humor—threatening to give it to the cat next door or enforcing vegetarianism. Charlie Brown, in turn, just wants a devoted dog, who'll be excited when he gets home, needs hugs, and doesn't spend so much time reliving World War I. "Whatever happened to the good old-fashioned neighborhood dog?" he wonders.

SECRET BOND
Snoopy doesn't easily admit that he appreciates Charlie Brown and only rarely shows him the love

◄ Back in 1950, when Snoopy was just a puppy, Charlie Brown would miss his "ol' pal," even overnight.

WHAT'S **WRONG** WITH YOU?

OTHER DOGS JUMP UP AND DOWN WHEN THEIR MASTERS COME HOME FROM SCHOOL...

THAT'S THE MOST SARCASTIC JUMPING UP AND DOWN I'VE EVER SEEN

▲ Sometimes Snoopy just isn't the dog that Charlie Brown wants him to be.

and affection he craves. He doesn't even remember his name, calling him "that round-headed kid." Deep down, Snoopy does love his owner and often goes to Charlie Brown for comfort—when his doghouse burns to the ground, he sleeps in Charlie Brown's bed while the renovations are being done. Charlie Brown, in turn, loves Snoopy. He misses him when he goes to camp or when Snoopy goes away (looking for his mom) and sometimes even at nighttime. Once, Charlie Brown quit school to look after Snoopy full time and make him happy (of course, Snoopy insists he was happy anyway).

SNOOPY'S FRIENDS

To most of the kids in the neighborhood, Snoopy is just Charlie Brown's weird dog. To self-obsessed Snoopy, they are merely his audience (and food bringers)—though when they clean his doghouse for him, he comments, "Isn't it nice to have friends." Peppermint Patty thinks he's a funny-looking kid with a big nose. Linus sees him as a rival (for his security blanket). For Lucy, he's a dancing and sparring partner (and she likes to beep his nose). But the bond that Snoopy has with Charlie Brown is different from all the others—and, actually, very special.

PEANUTS

I HOPE YOU ENJOYED YOUR DINNER, SIR

THIS EVENING WE HAVE THREE CHOICES FOR DESSERT... NOTHING, NOTHING, AND NOTHING!

11-7

HA HA HA HA

BONK!

▲ Charlie Brown likes to liven up the dull routine of daily dog feeding with a joke. But some jokes have a way of rebounding—with a BONK!

"[Snoopy] likes to think of himself as independent [but] without Charlie Brown, he couldn't survive."
—Charles M. Schulz

Happy Dance

Snoopy says "To live is to dance, to dance is to live" as his fluttering dancing feet lift him off the ground in sheer ecstasy. In a neighborhood full of insecurity, Snoopy is a rare being who can express such uncomplicated inner joy. He dances a duet with a falling leaf; he dances until his feet are sore; he dances in the snow; he dances an Indian summer dance (not that he's sure what that means);

he revels in his unfettered freedom with a "ha ha, you have to go to school and I don't" dance. His happy dance antagonizes mutual depressives Charlie Brown and Lucy: "What makes you think you're happy?" asks Charlie Brown, distrustingly, of Snoopy. Lucy comments, "Nobody could be that happy." But there's no stopping Snoopy and his uninhibited dancing joy.

> ## *"The whole world is coming apart, and you're dancing!"*
> —Lucy

DANCING DOG
Though undated, Schulz probably drew this sketch of Snoopy doing his happy dance in the late 1960s at one of his famous "chalk talks," where he would speak to audiences while sketching *Peanuts* characters.

STOP THE DANCE
In 1956, Snoopy began dancing for the first time, causing consternation for Lucy. Though she begins to get the dancing bug herself later. "If you can't lick 'em, join 'em!" she says.

FORGET YOUR TROUBLES
Snoopy and Linus dance without a care in the world, while Lucy acts as the disapproving voice of "reason." Linus provides his sister with an unanswerable response, to Snoopy's evident delight. It's dancing as deliberate dissidence!

FLEETING DANCE
Snoopy dances the briefest of duets with a falling leaf and expresses thanks for life's brief moments of joy.

Favorite Teacher

Linus thinks his favorite teacher, Miss Othmar, is a true gem. He also has some very odd notions about her.

▲ Exhausted after several days picketing, Miss Othmar falls to her knees, provoking an instant protective response in her disciple.

M iss Othmar is "the greatest teacher in the whole world," Linus believes. "A gem among gems." He doesn't worship her, though he is "very fond of the ground on which she walks." He is also convinced that she understands him, to which Lucy sneers, "Either she's a genius or she's new on the job." Linus makes grand speeches about her, talks to her in his sleep, and brings her flowers. But he is crushed when he learns that she considers security

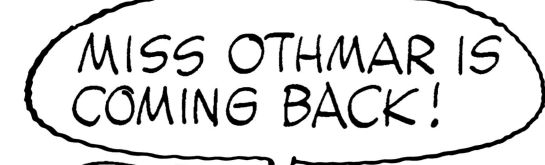

MISS OTHMAR IS COMING BACK!

◄ When Miss Othmar returns to teaching after leaving to get married, Linus is floating on air—literally.

"Children see more than we think they do, but at the same time almost never seem to know what is going on."
—Charles M. Schulz

▶ Linus is crushed when they fire his favorite teacher. His attitude to her replacement, Miss Halverson, borders on the insubordinate.

blankets a sign of immaturity. "Who's Miss Othmar?" he now says, coldly (clutching his beloved blanket). When we next meet Miss Othmar (not literally—she is never seen), Linus thinks he has upset her by repeatedly forgetting to bring in eggshells for an igloo-making project. "Poor Miss Othmar," he says. "I thought she was going to pass out." In fact, it turns out Miss Othmar has her mind on other things: the next day, when Linus actually remembers the eggshells, she isn't there. She has quit her job to get married. He sends her a wedding present: a box of eggshells.

THE RETURN OF MISS OTHMAR
A year later, in 1961, Miss Othmar returns to teaching. A newly infatuated Linus believes she teaches for free because she sees teaching as a "pure art form"—a single withering stare from Lucy is enough to strip him

of his innocence. A dark night of the soul follows, at the end of which Linus has convinced himself that, okay, she may get paid, but she hands it all back.

MISS OTHMAR ON STRIKE
Later that decade, Miss Othmar goes on strike. Linus goes to the picket line to offer support … and soup. He even risks becoming "involved" (Lucy's word) when he picks up the sign that she drops in her exhaustion. Then she is fired! A furious Linus writes a letter of protest … to the apostle Paul. Nevertheless, Miss Othmar is replaced by a new teacher, Miss Halverson, and Linus, being a stubborn "Othmarite," refuses to accept her—at least until Miss Halverson gives him the special task of pounding the chalkboard erasers. "My memories of Miss Othmar are going up in chalk dust," mourns a conflicted Linus.

▲ Linus is keen to let everyone know just how much he admires Miss Othmar, impressing even himself with his sincerity.

FIRST APPEARANCE

Linus's blanket first appears on
June 1, 1954. Lucy explains that
it gives him a sense of security.
Charlie Brown wonders if it
would work for him. (It doesn't.)

Portable Security

Linus's security blanket is made of one yard of flannel and absorbs all of his fears and frustrations. Since its first appearance in 1954, Linus has carried his blanket through the decades without shame or embarrassment. Yet everyone around him seems intent on depriving him of his "portable security." Linus even occasionally tries to rid himself of the addiction. Schulz had observed his own kids dragging around blankets or favorite toys, and, while he didn't invent the term "security blanket," he certainly popularized it.

MANY USES

Linus is proud of his blanket and its
additional uses, including a whip,
Dracula's cloak, a bullfighter's cape,
a hammock, a slingshot, felt for a
pool table, and many more.

FLYBY

Snoopy takes great
delight in running
at high speed past
Linus and grabbing
his security blanket
in his mouth.

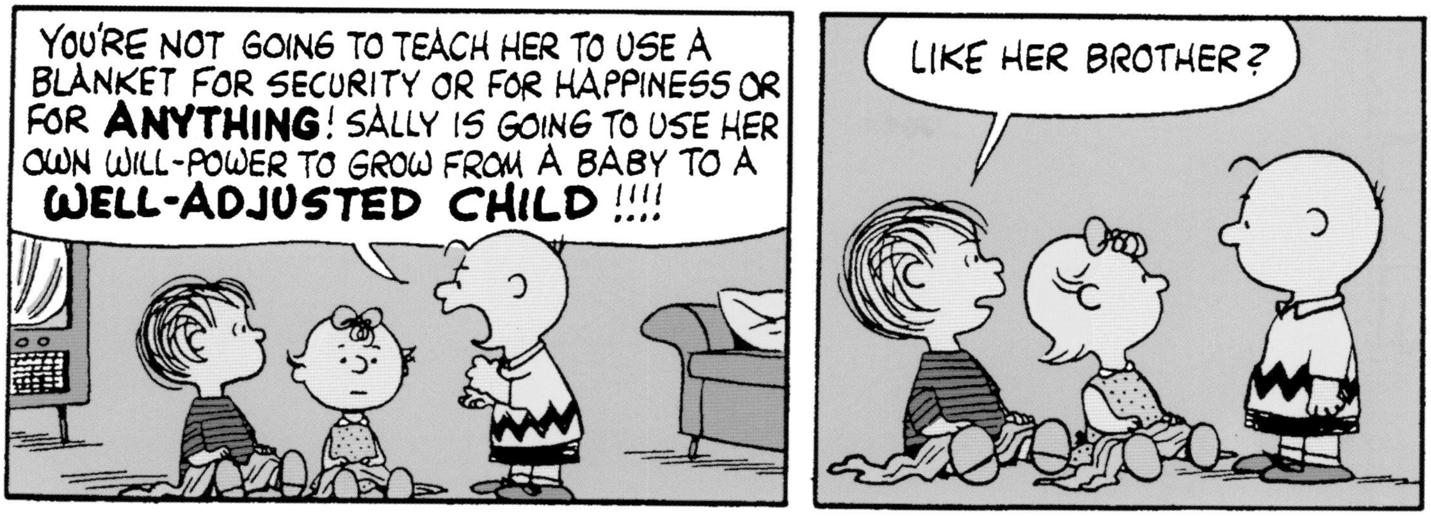
YOU'RE NOT GOING TO TEACH HER TO USE A BLANKET FOR SECURITY OR FOR HAPPINESS OR FOR ANYTHING! SALLY IS GOING TO USE HER OWN WILL-POWER TO GROW FROM A BABY TO A WELL-ADJUSTED CHILD!!!!
LIKE HER BROTHER?

SPREADING SECURITY

Linus tries to pass the habit onto Sally, crushing Charlie Brown's protests. Later, Sally finds the blanket a source of embarrassment, believing that no future husband of hers should be seen with one.

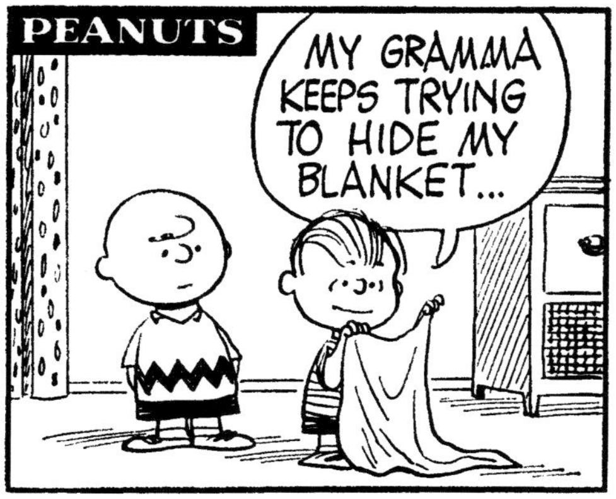
PEANUTS
MY GRAMMA KEEPS TRYING TO HIDE MY BLANKET...

OUTWITTING GRAMMA

Linus's interfering grandmother hides his blanket whenever she visits, but Linus has methods for outfoxing her: he lays out decoy blankets and disguises the real one as a bow tie.

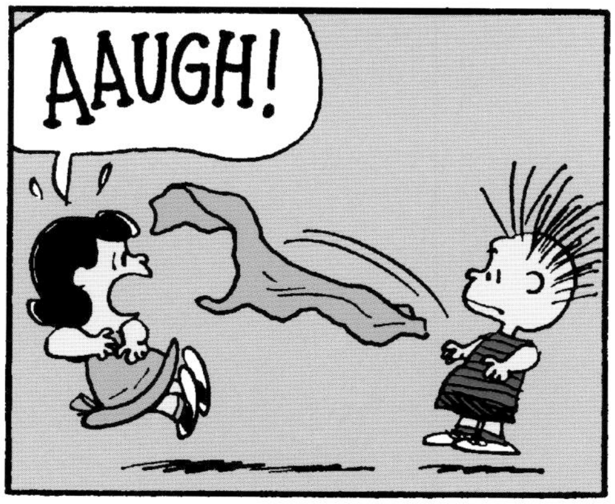
AAUGH!

BLANKET ATTACK

After years of stomping it, tromping it, and insulting it, Linus's blanket decides it's time to get its own back on Lucy—it hisses at her, creeps up on her, and attacks her!

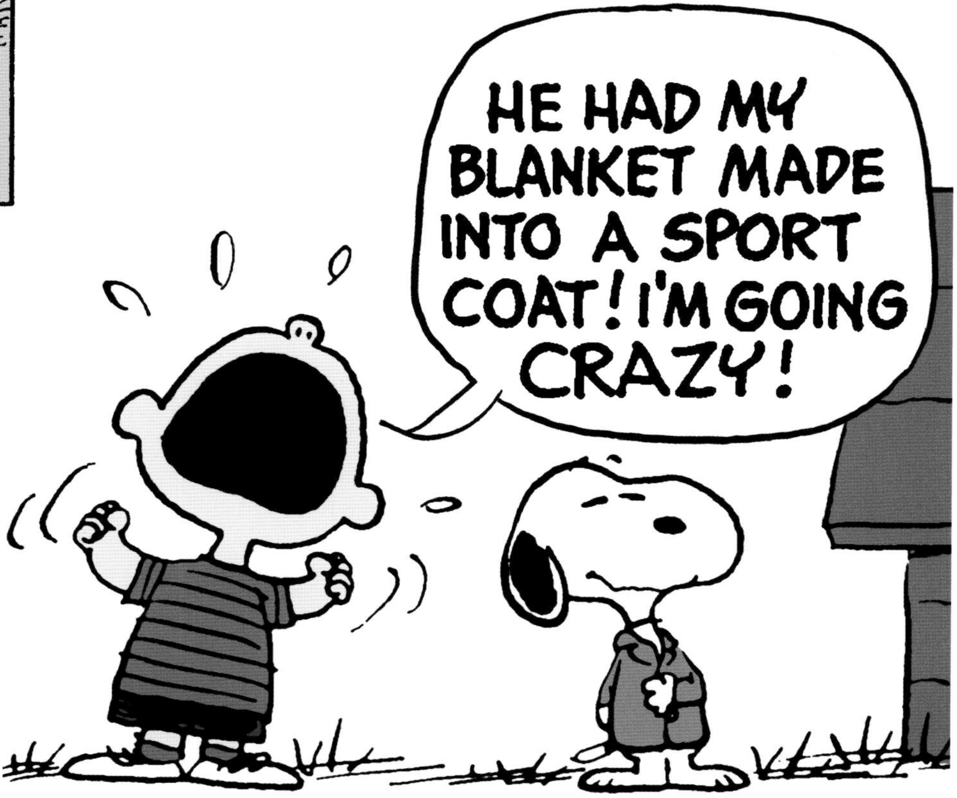
HE HAD MY BLANKET MADE INTO A SPORT COAT! I'M GOING CRAZY!

SECURITY COAT

Asked whether he plans to carry his blanket around his whole life, Linus suggested that he might have it made into a sport coat. But too late—Snoopy gets there first.

The Great Pumpkin

Linus believes the Great Pumpkin is one of childhood's most cherished beliefs—and Linus is his most loyal follower.

Ever since 1959, Linus has shunned trick-or-treating on Halloween to spend the night waiting for the arrival of the Great Pumpkin. According to Linus, the Great Pumpkin rises out of the most sincere pumpkin patch in the land with his big bag of toys for children who have been good. Linus diligently writes letters to the Great Pumpkin, sings pumpkin carols, and sends pumpkin cards (or would if he could find a store that sells them).

DENOMINATIONAL DIFFERENCES

Schulz said that Linus, "who is bright but innocent," was "confusing Halloween with Christmas because he was one holiday ahead of himself." Linus believes the Great Pumpkin is "fulfilling a moral obligation," whereas Santa Claus treats it as just a job. A "denominational squabble," comments Charlie Brown. The trouble is that Linus waits in his "sincere"

pumpkin patch each year, only to be disillusioned when the Great Pumpkin doesn't show. He often wrestles with a crisis of belief and decides not to believe in the Great Pumpkin anymore—only to try again the next year with renewed faith. Linus suffers for his belief, too. Not only does he forgo the candy bars and cookies he would get by trick-or-treating, though Lucy sometimes saves him some, he even loses the chance to become school president after he makes a speech about the Great Pumpkin and nearly loses Charlie Brown as a friend when they have a spat.

SPREADING THE WORD

Linus tries to spread the gospel of the Great Pumpkin. Though not a believer, Charlie Brown waits in the pumpkin patch with him one year when the Great Pumpkin appears—but it turns out only to be Snoopy. Lucy mocks his gullibility and, always

◄ Sally will do almost anything for her "sweet babboo," even sit out in a cold pumpkin patch at night.

THIS IS THE TIME OF YEAR WHEN WE ALL WRITE TO THE "GREAT PUMPKIN," AND TELL HIM WHAT WE WANT FOR HALLOWEEN

▲ Linus first starts writing to the Great Pumpkin. He is surprised he even has to explain to Lucy what he's doing.

the entrepreneur, starts her own "insincere" pumpkin patch by selling the pumpkins. One year, Linus persuades Sally to wait with him—she is furious when the Great Pumpkin doesn't appear. Peppermint Patty does become a "disciple" because, according to her, she's trusting, faithful, superstitious, and a "little bit stupid." In any case, she blows it by faking a pumpkin patch with pumpkins bought from a fruit stand. Marcie wants to believe in the "Great Squash" (she struggles with the name) but her parents "deprogram" her: apparently it's okay to believe in Santa Claus but wrong to believe in the "Great Grape." Linus may be a "false prophet." But he's truly sincere!

▲ Figurine illustrating "determination," with Lucy encountering Linus asleep in the pumpkin patch—again!

"Linus gives to the Great Pumpkin those qualities Santa Claus is supposed to have."
—Charles M. Schulz

▲ In 1968, Hallmark Greeting Cards released a greeting-card booklet of Linus' pumpkin carols to celebrate the season.

▶ Linus faints at the first near sighting of the Great Pumpkin, which turns out to be "just a used dog" named Snoopy.

WHAT HAPPENED? DID I FAINT? WHAT DID HE LEAVE US? DID HE LEAVE US ANY TOYS?

NO TOYS... JUST A USED DOG...

▲ Lucy has a blunt response to Charlie Brown's admission of "deep feelings of depression," in the first appearance of the psychiatric booth on March 27, 1959.

The Doctor Is In

Lucy will treat any patient who has a problem … and a nickel.

Children have long sold lemonade from stands outside of their houses. Schulz updated the lemonade stand to a psychiatry stand, with Lucy offering psychiatric advice. Her credentials? "I know everything!" Her true motivation? "Plink! The beautiful sound of beautiful plinking nickels!"

DOCTOR-PATIENT RELATIONSHIPS

Charlie Brown is Lucy's most regular customer, seeking advice on everything from feeling depressed to feeling that life is passing him by. "Well, live in it then!" shouts Lucy. Her most common diagnosis is "Snap out of it!" which, according to Schulz, was his mother-in-law's answer to any complaint. Lucy also treats Linus for pantophobia (the fear of everything) and Schroeder for depression at the thought of Beethoven's deafness. She advises Pigpen to see an archaeologist instead of a psychiatrist. Snoopy pays her in dog food! Sometimes, Lucy employs an assistant, including a glasses-wearing Snoopy and Schroeder, whose advice to his patients is to "go home and listen to

◄ For Lucy, psychiatry is an exact science: the patient owes her exactly five cents. This undated sketch was probably drawn at one of Schulz's famous "chalk talks" in the late 1960s.

▲ Lucy's system for pointing out Charlie Brown's faults is unique and for his own good. She has prepared slides dealing with his physical, personal, and inherited faults. His biggest and most damaging faults are shown in color.

▲ Snoopy sets up a rival stand, undercutting Lucy on price and offering a friendlier service.

▲ Linus's musings on the possible meanings of Lucy's THE DOCTOR IS IN sign results in a sudden termination of the session.

a Brahms quartet." Lucy's advice is usually useless, but occasionally almost profound. She once told Charlie Brown that life is like a grocery cart, "and the world is our supermarket." Charlie Brown concludes he has six items or less. Occasionally the advice comes in the form of a punch in the patient's face. Lucy sometimes needs to visit a psychiatrist herself, playing the role of both patient and doctor.

FRIENDLY COMPETITION
In 1964, Schulz said he kept up with "the latest on neuroses and phobias" and that "everyone is a

lay psychiatrist." Lucy, too, keeps up with the changing times, offering "Psychiatry à Go-Go!" in 1965 and advice on "self-actualization" in 1970. In 1967, she raises her prices to "winter rates" of seven cents and in 1981 increases her fee to 50 cents due to rising inflation. However, she sometimes has competition. In 1966, Snoopy sets up his own "Hug a Warm Puppy" stand (a bargain at one cent), and, in 1968, offers "Friendly Hugs" for two cents. You may ask, as Franklin does, is Lucy a real doctor? As Lucy would answer, "Was the lemonade ever any good?"

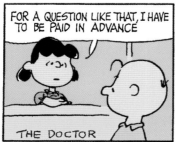

▲ Lucy demonstrates that she does have an understanding of psychology after all.

The Head Beagle

Sir? Judge? Father of Us All? Even Snoopy isn't sure how to address the Head Beagle!

In Snoopy's world, every dog respects and fears the Head Beagle. No dog wants to be reported to the Head Beagle. A mere letter from the Head Beagle is enough to make a dog faint. Being summoned to appear before the Head Beagle can bring shame on a dog's whole family. So when Frieda reports Snoopy to the Head Beagle for not chasing enough rabbits, poor Snoopy has a sleepless night and wears black to his appointment.

SNOOPY'S PROMOTION
The Head Beagle has presidential powers and can charge a dog for not chasing enough rabbits per month. Luckily, in Snoopy's case, the Head Beagle is very understanding. In fact, a few months later, Snoopy is selected for a secret assignment (so secret we never find out what it is). Later, he receives even greater news: he has

been promoted to Head Beagle. Snoopy doesn't last long though—the responsibilities are too much for him and he absconds from his post, hiding out at Peppermint Patty's house.

FINAL MISSION
In October 1972, Snoopy goes on one last mission for the Head Beagle. He receives a coded letter: three paw prints. Deciphered, it means "Thompson

▲ The job of head beagle is too much for Snoopy. Everyone wants something. Everyone complains. He works day and night and no one appreciates it!

◄ Becoming Head Beagle is the proudest day of Charlie Brown's life—he even serves Snoopy's dinner in a special bowl. "How gauche," comments Snoopy, "but nice."

is in trouble." Snoopy knows just what to do. Disguising his identity with his "famous" fake moustache, Snoopy sets off to find "that stupid Thompson." His search takes him through city streets, shady restaurants, and dark forests. But too late—poor Thompson! Snoopy writes up his report to the Head

Beagle: "Subject attempted to subdue ten thousand rabbits by himself. End came quickly. Rabbit-tat-tat and it was all over." In a postscript, Snoopy lets slip what really happened: the rabbits made Thompson an offer he couldn't refuse—like "Don" Vito Corleone in that year's hit film, *The Godfather*.

▲ Snoopy patrols the school playground on his first top-secret mission for the Head Beagle. When he is chased off the premises, Snoopy grumbles that "the principal does NOT outrank the Head Beagle."

▲ Snoopy sets off on his assignment for the Head Beagle. If he can just get to Thompson before "they" do!

◄ The mayor of Los Angeles, Sam Yorty, presented Schulz with a congratulatory certificate saluting Snoopy's new elevated position.

▲ Linus's theory that the Head Beagle and the Great Pumpkin are one and the same is "ridiculous" according to Snoopy.

Snoopy's Daily Dozen

In 1961, President John F. Kennedy initiated a drive to improve America's fitness, especially among schoolchildren. He wanted to spark a national fitness awareness and encourage schools to support fitness as well as sport skills. His program was supported by a national print, radio, and television publicity campaign. Charles Schulz got involved, too, creating a special exercise booklet, *Snoopy's Daily Dozen: 12 Physical Fitness Exercises*, which was issued by Hallmark. The original artworks shown here belonged to Arnold Shapiro, a former writer, then editor, with Hallmark, who had first reached out to Schulz to ask about designing a line of Hallmark greetings cards. Shapiro and Schulz became friends, and Shapiro donated part of his collection to the Charles M. Schulz Museum in California.

SNOOPY'S DAILY DOZEN

12 PHYSICAL FITNESS EXERCISES

BY CHARLES SCHULZ

BOOKLET COVER
Snoopy shows off his muscles on the cover. The phrase "daily dozen" was originally an exercise program invented for soldiers in World War I and became a craze in the 1920s and 1930s.

LEG EXTENSION

Charlie Brown demonstrates a "Leg Extension" in this unpublished page—while Snoopy looks less than convinced.

BEAR AND INCHWORM WALKS

The exercises in the booklet included imitating a number of animals, including the bear, inchworm, kangaroo, crab, and gorilla.

RISE AND SHINE

Frieda attempts to motivate Snoopy to exercise in this unpublished title page.

HELPING HANDS

This unpublished page shows Violet and Patty doing the "Pull Stretcher."

The Little Red-Haired Girl

▲ Charlie Brown hides behind the tree outside the Little Red-Haired Girl's house—hoping he'll see her!

As Charlie Brown says, "Nothing takes the taste out of peanut butter like unrequited love."

Charlie Brown's great unrequited love is a girl who is never actually seen in the strip. Chuck always refers to her as the Little Red-Haired Girl; he never uses her real name. He longs to meet her, though he never plucks up the courage to do so. She is first mentioned in a melancholy Sunday strip in 1961. Charlie Brown is spending school lunch hour alone, and we hear his thoughts: he notices the paint on the bench he's sitting on, he appreciates his peanut butter sandwiches, and, fleetingly, he wishes the girl with red hair would sit with him. There's no punch line. Over the years, Charlie Brown wrestles many times with his shyness and insecurity. He imagines all sorts of scenarios where he would talk to her, even go riding with her on ponies! He tries writing letters to her, but crumples up each one. He dreams about her. Even when he gets paired with her on a science project, he can't bring himself to initiate a conversation. Linus and Lucy are both able to talk to her—Linus even tells her outright that Charlie

> THAT LITTLE RED-HAIRED GIRL IS WATCHING, AND I'M GOING TO PITCH A GREAT GAME, AND SHE'S GOING TO BE IMPRESSED, AND...

▲ When the Little Red-Haired Girl watches the ball game, Charlie Brown starts trembling so much he has to be sent home. In his absence, his team wins the game.

▶ Charlie Brown writes to the Little Red-Haired Girl—but then, as he says, a lot of great letters never get mailed.

Dear Little Red Haired Girl, I love you very much.

◄ The Little Red-Haired Girl is depicted in the strip for the first time, in silhouette—fox-trotting with a beagle.

Brown is madly in love with her. When the Little Red-Haired Girl moves away in 1969, Linus desperately pushes Charlie Brown to speak to her before it's too late. It's one of the few times that Linus gets genuinely angry at his friend, shouting, "You never do anything! All you ever do is just stand there! I'm so mad I could scream! I AM screaming!!"

REAL-LIFE INSPIRATION
The identity of the real-life inspiration for the Little Red-Haired Girl came to light only in 1990—the 40th anniversary of the strip—though Schulz had first hinted at it in 1975. In 1950, he had dated a red-haired woman who worked in accounting at Art Instruction Inc., named Donna Mae Johnson. "I just thought she was wonderful," Schulz said. Donna, however, had another admirer, Alan Wold, whom she had known since school. Alan finally proposed to her and she accepted. When he was 75, Schulz said, "You never do get over your first love."

▲ Charles Schulz with the Little Red-Haired Girl, Donna Johnson, in April 1950.

> ## "Each of us can imagine what she must look like better than I can draw her."
> —Charles M. Schulz

▲ Charlie Brown mentions the little girl with red hair for the first time.

► Charlie Brown has another sleepless night as he wrestles with paradoxes.

Is Happiness a Warm Puppy?

◀ This figurine, issued by Determined Productions Inc. in 1971, reminds us that "Happiness is having someone to lean on."

I n a strip that appeared on April 25, 1960, Lucy pats and hugs Snoopy, concluding with great satisfaction, "Happiness is a warm puppy."
The strip caught the eye of Connie Boucher, whose licensing company Determined Productions Inc. had started working with Schulz on *Peanuts* merchandise. She pitched an idea to make a picture book inspired by the strip. Though Schulz was not initially convinced, that same day he sat down at his desk and drew enough variations to fill a whole book.

BESTSELLER

Published in the fall of 1962, *Happiness Is a Warm Puppy* was a massive hit, sitting on the bestseller lists for 43 weeks and, by 1967, selling 1.3 million copies in multiple languages. The format would now be called a gift book, but at the time it was unusual: small and square, relatively high priced, with unnumbered, colorful pages, each with a single simple illustration and an accompanying thought on the theme of simple pleasures. The book's "little moments" (as Schulz put it) charmed the public at a time of uneasiness: the Cuban missile crisis had just brought the United States to the brink of nuclear war.

CULTURAL MEME

The phrase "happiness is …" became part of the zeitgeist, used on everything from bumper stickers to protest banners—it is even referenced by the 1968 Beatles song, "Happiness Is a Warm Gun"—and spawned an industry of follow-ups and other merchandise.

WHAT'S SO HAPPY ABOUT A WARM PUPPY?

◀▲ Linus remains a skeptic. After all, what's a warm puppy when you have a blanket?

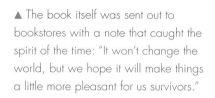

▲ The book itself was sent out to bookstores with a note that caught the spirit of the time: "It won't change the world, but we hope it will make things a little more pleasant for us survivors."

HAPPINESS IS A WARM PUPPY

▲ Charlie Brown and Snoopy share a special moment in a lithograph from 1993 that Schulz created using ink and watercolor.

► The success of the first title inspired a number of sequels. *Security Is a Thumb and a Blanket* was the number-two bestselling nonfiction book of 1963. Between them, these three alone would sell 800,000 copies!

▲ The strip that spawned a phrase and a craze. Next time Lucy tries to cuddle Snoopy, he thinks "PHOOEY!" and backs off.

Awards and Honors

By 1954, *Peanuts* had already begun to take off, with ever-increasing numbers of readers in the United States and elsewhere via foreign and foreign-language newspapers, and in particular with students in campuses across the country who felt a kinship with the strip's existential angst. By 1956, the strip had 20 million readers and official recognition began: the *Saturday Evening Post* ran the first major profile of Schulz and the National Cartoonists Society awarded him the prestigious Reuben Award for Outstanding Cartoonist of the Year in 1955. Schulz made the trip to New York to receive the award from the 77-year-old master cartoonist Reuben "Rube" Goldberg

himself at the Astor Hotel. In 1964, he received the award for a second time, the first time in the society's history that any cartoonist had done so. In 1965, *Time* magazine ran a cover story on "The World According to Peanuts," with art specially drawn by Schulz. In 1966, Schulz won an Emmy for Outstanding Children's Program for the animated TV special, *A Charlie Brown Christmas*. In 1967, *Peanuts* appeared on the cover of *Life* magazine, after which Schulz's fame was so widespread, he was no longer able to keep up his habit of personally answering fan letters and requests for drawings. Much more recognition and many more awards would follow over the years.

REUBEN AWARD
The National Cartoonists Society trophy for Outstanding Cartoonist of the Year is a bronze-cast statuette, designed by Rube Goldberg, depicting four cartoon figures beneath an ink bottle.

TWICE-HONORED
Schulz pictured with his second Reuben Award in 1964.

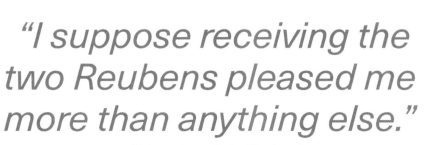

"I suppose receiving the two Reubens pleased me more than anything else."
—Charles M. Schulz

KEY TO THE CITY

In June 1968, the mayor of San Francisco, Joseph Alioto, presented Schulz with an ornamental "key to the city." In 1985, he was awarded this second key, by Mayor Diane Feinstein. Made of cast iron, it has a gold medallion mounted in the handle.

CONGRESSIONAL MEDAL

In the year of his death, Schulz was awarded the highest honor the US Congress can bestow on a civilian: the Congressional Gold Medal.

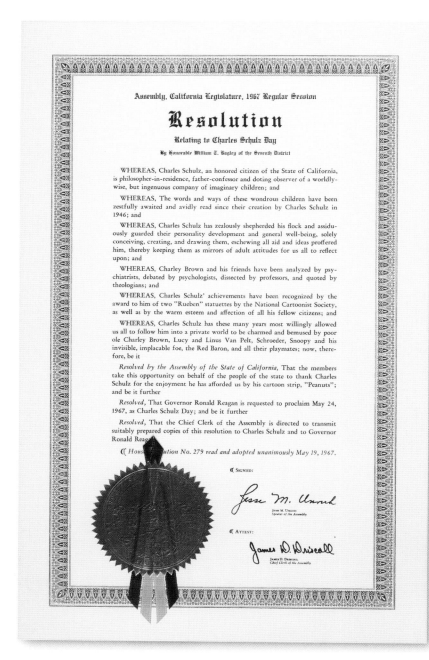

CHARLES M. SCHULZ DAY

This scroll presented to Schulz in 1967 by California governor Ronald Reagan proclaims May 24 Charles M. Schulz Day in honor of the success of *Peanuts*.

ELZIE SEGAR AWARD

In 1980, Schulz received the National Cartoonists Society's Elzie Segar Award. Named for the creator of one of Schulz's favorite comic strips, *Popeye*, the award honors Schulz for his "outstanding contributions to the art of cartooning."

The Girl with Naturally Curly Hair

▲ Frieda can't concentrate on playing baseball when she's worrying about foreign policy.

BONK!

Frieda prides herself on being a conversationalist and having naturally curly hair.

◄ Frieda was modeled on Schulz's friend, Frieda Rich, from Art Instruction Inc., who had dark curly hair and described herself as a good conversationalist.

In March 1961, Linus introduces the gang to the girl who sits behind him in class. He forgets to say that he hasn't heard a word the teacher has said all semester. That's because Frieda likes to talk, introducing a barrage of random conversation starters from how lousy television programs are to how little she reads. She also manages to mention her hair in every conversation—it's naturally curly, you know.

FRIEDA'S FOIBLES

Frieda is one of the few girls who are generally nice to Charlie Brown. She joins his baseball team, but refuses to wear a cap in case it prevents spectators from seeing her hair. She is also tolerant of Linus's security blanket—though the "constant slurping" of his thumb-sucking nauseates her. She irritates Lucy by leaning on Schroeder's piano and pretending she knows anything at all about Beethoven. Her main problem is Snoopy, whom she thinks is lazy because he doesn't chase rabbits. By the end of the decade, Frieda had dropped into the background, Schulz commenting tersely that she "added relatively little to the strip."

◄ Frieda buys a cat called Faron in an attempt to show up Snoopy. However, Faron proves to be even lazier than Snoopy!

▲ Linus meets 5 for the first time. Linus thinks, if we all had numbers for names, every Tom, Dick, and Harry would be named 3.1416.

Numbers and More Numbers

Meet 5 and his sisters, 4 and 3. Their dad gave them numbers instead of names.

I n 1963, Schulz introduced a new character. His full name is 555, but everyone calls him 5 for short. His sisters are called 4 and 3. "Nice feminine names," comments Charlie Brown wryly. Their surname is 95472, which is actually their zip code—and Schulz's too, for Sebastopol, California, where he was then living. Five-digit zip codes were introduced in the United States for the first time in July 1963, and, it seems, this even proved too much for 5's dad, who was already disturbed by all the numbers "put on us these days." Hysterical, he decided that everyone in his family should have a number instead of a name. "His way of protesting, huh?" asks Lucy. "No," replies 5, "this is his way of giving in!"

NUMERICAL CONFUSION

Having numbers for names leads to all sorts of problems. Snoopy isn't sure if his name is V or 5, and 5's teacher always mispronounces his surname. She puts the accent on the 2 instead of on the 4—embarrassing! Sally's first thought on meeting 5 is "Mrs. Sally 95472," but then she decides she "can't see it!"

◀ In time, 5 becomes one of the gang, playing on the baseball team and visiting Lucy's psychiatry booth with the rest of 'em.

▲ Lucy meets 4 and 3 for the first time. Snoopy later comments, "The next thing you know, kids won't be born. You'll just have to send in for them."

Curse You, Red Baron!

Snoopy's greatest and longest-lived persona takes to the skies: the World War I Flying Ace.

In October 1965, Snoopy puts on a flying helmet and begins his adventures as the World War I Flying Ace. His doghouse becomes the Sopwith Camel, a model of British biplane fighter aircraft that first saw action in 1917. His archenemy is the dreaded Red Baron. Though never depicted in the strip, the Red Baron was a real fighter pilot in the German Air Force during World War I:

Manfred von Richthofen, who had noble ancestry and painted his Fokker triplane red, hence the nickname. Richthofen won 80 aerial victories in the war, more than any other pilot. Schulz credited the inspiration for Snoopy's Flying Ace persona to his son Monte, who at age 13 was interested in making World War I model airplanes. A visit from Monte to Schulz's drawing studio with his latest model plane resulted in Schulz sketching Snoopy with a little helmet and sitting on top of his doghouse. Then he asked Monte to get one of his books about World War I planes. "I thumbed through until we found the name—Sopwith Camel. And that's how it started."

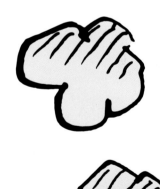

◄ In a leather flying hat, goggles, and a dashing red scarf, Snoopy is the handsome, heartbreaking World War I Flying Ace.

▲ Snoopy is "captured by the enemy" when Charlie Brown takes him to the vet for a shot.

▲ This wooden music box, featuring Snoopy wearing a felt flight helmet sitting on his yellow doghouse, was issued by Schmid in 1968.

▲ High over France, Snoopy thinks he's got the Red Baron—but too late! He hates that Red Baron!

WARTIME ADVENTURES

How it started for Snoopy was a simple greeting to his team—"Good morning, ground crew!"—and a quick pose beside his Sopwith Camel (the Flying Ace is very famous) and the hunt for the Red Baron is on. Linus interrupts Snoopy's fantasy this first time—shouting "Rat A Tat Tat Tat Tat Tat Tat" behind him. But soon Snoopy is acting out fully fledged wartime crusades: aerial dogfights, being shot down behind enemy lines, and lonesome nights spent drinking root beer in a café in France—in his mind, he's escaped the secure suburban world of the rest of the strip.

"I knew I had one of the best things I had thought of in a long time."
—Charles M. Schulz

▲ Marcie becomes a willing participant in Snoopy's World War I adventures.

DASHING PILOT
Snoopy poses
for a snapshot—his
ground crew like
to send pictures of
him to "their girls
back home."

Curse this Stupid War!

Snoopy's adventures as the Flying Ace became—and continue to be—a cultural phenomenon. Snoopy managed to be both a symbol of wartime heroics and a satire on them. His battles with the Red Baron inspired fighter squadrons in the Vietnam War, which used Snoopy's image as a mascot, and found approval in the 1960s counterculture—a psychedelic rock band from San Francisco took the name Sopwith Camel. He has also inspired a massive array of toys and other merchandise. In response to the strips, many veterans from the war wrote to Schulz. Some even sent him photographs of real places where Snoopy had flown, such as Pont-à-Mousson, in northeastern France. The cartoonist then used these photos to authenticate Snoopy's further adventures. But what will the Flying Ace do when the war is over? Probably a little barnstorming, Snoopy thinks.

CIVILIAN LIFE
The retired Flying Ace takes
Schroeder to summer camp, with
Marcie as the flight attendant.

DERRING-DO
The Flying Ace makes a
daring dash across barbed
wire–strewn no-man's-land.

UNEXPECTED ENCOUNTER

In disguise, Snoopy meets the Red Baron in the first of many encounters. Later, Snoopy will ask for his autograph. The Red Baron, in turn, sends Snoopy a get-well card.

HIT ALBUM

In 1968, a US rock group, the Royal Guardsmen, sold three million copies of a hit single called "Snoopy vs. the Red Baron." A string of sequels and LPs followed.

NEW YEAR'S RAID

The Flying Ace has one weakness—root beer!

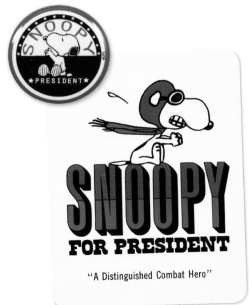

COMBAT HERO

In the 1968 presidential campaign, voters actually put Snoopy's name down on ballot papers as a write-in candidate!

FLYING COIN BANK

This papier-mâché coin bank from 1977 features Snoopy as the Flying Ace piloting an orange plane.

PEANUTS

TAKE IT EASY NOW...DON'T BE FRIGHTENED..YOU'LL FIND A LOT OF YOUR FRIENDS HERE..

LEAVES **NEED** ME! I HELP THEM THROUGH WHAT IS REALLY THE BIG EMOTIONAL PERIOD OF THEIR LIVES!

WHEN A LEAF FALLS FROM A TREE, HE'S ALONE..HE'S LIKE A PERSON LEAVING THE COUNTRY, AND MOVING TO A STRANGE CITY..

I'M KIND OF A "WELCOME-WAGON" FOR LEAVES!

FRIEND TO LEAVES
Linus talks to leaves in the fall. Snoopy does, too.

Seasonal Celebrations

S chulz lived much of his adult life in California, with its relatively unvarying climate. His strip, however, reflected his upbringing in the Midwest, with marked seasons. With a daily strip, Schulz was able to provide a connection to his daily readership as they moved through the year together.

YEARLY RITUALS

The *Peanuts* year begins with New Year's celebrations, followed by winter ice-skating and snowman building. Valentine's Day sees Charlie Brown mourning his empty mailbox (unless Snoopy's inside it). Easter is heralded by the Easter Beagle and the start of baseball

DELIVERING EGGS
Each year, the Easter Beagle delivers Easter eggs to everyone (though he runs out just before he reaches Charlie Brown).

SURPRISE SMAK
At least someone loves Charlie Brown enough to give him a Valentine's Day kiss on the nose.

HALLOWEEN NIGHT
The gang go trick-or-treating. Charlie Brown had trouble with the scissors and cut too many holes in his ghost sheet.

season. School's out for the summer in June—meaning summer camp for some and fun in paddling pools and at the beach for others. Back to school causes panic, particularly in Sally ("Put on the boiled eggs! Shine your shoes! Make your lunch! Conjugate your verbs!"). Linus and Snoopy talk to the falling leaves in fall. Then it's Halloween (look out for the Great Pumpkin), followed by snow again, which only means one thing: Beethoven's birthday. Oh, and Christmas!

NEW YEAR'S EVE
Snoopy starts the year with a sore head after "chug-a-lugging" root beer at Woodstock's New Year's party.

5   **SEASONAL GIFTS**
1 Valentine's Day plate, Schmid Company (1979) **2** Easter Beagle, Determined Productions Inc. (1990) **3** Christmas bell, Schmid Company (1975) **4** Snow globe, Department 56 (2005) **5** Halloween pumpkin train, Danbury Mint (c.2000)

Summer Camp

▲ Peppermint Patty and Marcie first meet at summer camp.

Summer camp provides opportunities to make new friends and miss the ones back home.

Charlie Brown first goes to camp in June 1965. He starts off dreading it, just as Schulz did as a child; he remembered having "absolutely no desire to be sent away to a summer camp." Drawing on his wartime memories, he described it as the "equivalent to being drafted." Schulz's experience of being shipped out to army camp for training in 1943 immediately after his mother's funeral must have been traumatic for him. Not having had the time to grieve properly, he said, "The first few days— maybe a week or so—I was totally alone." He described dropping all of that loneliness "heavily upon poor Charlie Brown."

INTO THE FRAY
In fact, camp isn't as bad as Charlie Brown fears. Just as Schulz himself was "big-brothered" at army training camp by a sympathetic corporal, Elmer Roy Hagemeyer, Charlie Brown finds someone to bond with: a boy called Roy. It is Charlie Brown who does the big-brothering, as Roy is lonelier at first than even he is. He cheers Roy up and feels proud that he "really helped someone." Though, of course, there's a downside: his baseball team wins their first-ever game while he is away!

▶ In keeping with Schulz's idea that summer camp is like boot camp, even Charlie Brown's cap resembles the side caps worn by American GIs in the 1940s.

◄ Leaving for camp for the first time in 1965, Charlie Brown feels like a soldier going to war.

CAMP EXPERIENCES

Over the following years, Charlie Brown goes to camp many times, occasionally with Snoopy (as the World War I Flying Ace). Linus also goes, meeting Roy again, and being elected camp president after enlightening everyone about the Great Pumpkin. Roy is also the connector between Charlie Brown and a new character who lives in Roy's neighborhood: Peppermint Patty. Being sporty and outgoing, she loves camp—and arranges baseball games that give Charlie Brown a chance to be struck out there as well as at home.

◄ Peppermint Patty meets Sophie, Clara, and Shirley, who turn out to be lonely at camp, until they meet the "keen little kid from the boys' camp across the lake"—Snoopy in Flying Ace mode.

▲ Linus spreads the word around the campfire—and ends up staying an extra week after being elected camp president.

► Charlie Brown masters his own feelings of loneliness to help Roy.

The Rare Gem

Peppermint Patty is a star athlete, a poor student, and her father's "rare gem."

NO, MA'AM, I DIDN'T WEAR A DRESS TODAY BECAUSE I'VE DECIDED TO DEFY THE DRESS CODE

▲ Peppermint Patty makes a stand against the school rule that girls must wear a dress.

Patricia Reichardt, known to all as "Peppermint" Patty, met Charlie Brown in 1966 through a mutual friend, Roy, who lives in Patty's neighborhood across town and went to camp with Charlie Brown and Linus. She is a confident, witty girl—"a take-charge guy" in her words—who excels at sports. She tries to show Charlie Brown's baseball team how to win, until she realizes it's hopeless. Her weakness is school, where she struggles with homework and tests and repeatedly falls asleep at her desk. She blames this on the fact that she stays up late waiting for her single-parent dad to come home from work. She and her dad have a close relationship: he calls her his "rare gem" (a phrase Schulz himself called his youngest daughter, Jill). Her dad also gave her the sandals that she wears every day; she even fought the school authorities when they tried to ban sandals and make her wear a dress. Schulz described her as "forthright, doggedly loyal, with a devastating singleness of purpose."

FRIENDSHIPS
Underneath her bravado, Peppermint Patty has a vulnerable side. She is insecure about her looks, believing that she has a big

◀ Peppermint Patty "goes through life with blinders on," according to Schulz. "This can be wonderful at times but also disastrous."

◄ Peppermint Patty asks Snoopy to go to the school dance with her. She has a great time until some kid asks about her "weird lookin' boyfriend." She hits him and gets asked to leave.

▲ Peppermint Patty is fond of Charlie Brown, even though he "doesn't possess any of the characteristics she respects," according to Schulz.

nose. Though Snoopy, who she thinks is just a "funny-looking kid," has a bigger one! She develops a crush on Charlie Brown, or "Chuck" as she calls him, and tries to entice him into admitting feelings for her. He likes her as a friend, but remains oblivious to her as a potential girlfriend. She chats to Linus about her crush on Charlie Brown and often waits for the arrival of the Great Pumpkin with him.

INSPIRATION

Schulz felt that Peppermint Patty was a "good addition" who could "almost carry another strip by herself." He created the character to fit the name, which had been inspired by a dish of candy sitting in his living room. He also felt that Peppermint Patty's best friend, Marcie, had been a good addition to the strip—but she wouldn't enter it until 1971.

▲ Peppermint Patty comes across town to meet "Chuck Brown" and his baseball team. She believes he needs a "take-charge guy."

► Peppermint Patty doesn't understand school. She has a better time when she signs up for the Ace Obedience School (for dogs!).

Peppermint Patty's Neighborhood

Peppermint Patty lives in an area with its own diverse range of characters, including one of the strip's few bullies: Thibault. Nevertheless, Peppermint Patty is unfailingly supportive of her gang. She sets up their baseball team, with star player, José Peterson, who is half Mexican and half Swedish (his mom has Peppermint Patty over for tortillas and Swedish meatballs). She also organizes a football team, plays hockey, and figure-skates. She goes to school with Marcie, Roy, and the strip's first African-American character, Franklin, introduced in 1968.

NEW PLAYER
New character José Peterson came to Schulz in a dream. "Why in the world I had such a dream and would think of such a name as José Peterson is a mystery to me," he said.

PEPPERMINT PATTY'S TEAM
Peppermint Patty's baseball team includes herself as manager, star player José Peterson, Thibault at second base, Franklin in center, and, on borrowed time, Marcie.

FOOTBALL TEAM

Peppermint Patty coaches a football team in her neighborhood, with local players Franklin and Roy.

KEEPING IN TOUCH

Peppermint Patty stays in touch with the goings-on in Charlie Brown's neighborhood by phone.

TOUGH ATTITUDE

Surly Thibault has a tough-guy mullet and sideburns—and a very large chip on his shoulder!

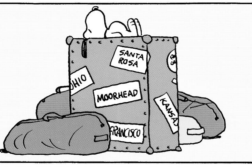

AWAY GAME

Charlie Brown's team makes the long-haul journey to Peppermint Patty's neighborhood.

From the Drawing Board

Schulz's original four-panel daily strips were drawn on predivided templates with panels that were 5½ inches (14 cm) high and 6½ inches (17 cm) wide. "This makes for quite a large panel," Schulz said, "but I need the working space to be able to get the proper expressions and make my lettering clear." The strips were then reduced in size for publication.

By the end of his career, he had a smaller rectangular template of 19 x 5½ inches (48 x 14 cm) that he could divide into panels however he wished. Schulz explained, "I have to work large in order that the pen lines can be made bold enough to stand this reduction." This strip, which appeared March 8, 1966, showed the bird who would become Woodstock.

The *Peanuts* title was preprinted.

Schulz would occasionally gift his original comic strips to friends, colleagues, fans, and charities.

Schulz dated each strip with the month and day, working approximately six weeks ahead of schedule.

Schulz would paste the copyright line in an inconspicuous spot in the comic strip.

"I have found drawing with pen and ink to be very challenging as well as gratifying. I feel that it is possible to achieve something near to what fine artists call 'paint quality' when working with a pen."
—Charles M. Schulz

Strips were drawn on Strathmore three-ply paper with India ink.

Daily strip templates were predivided into four panels.

When a batch of strips was finished, Schulz would fold them in half and send them by mail to United Feature Syndicate.

Schulz usually signed each strip in one of the corners of the last panel.

Grade-A Student

Franklin is cool and collected. But it's not always easy being an A-grade student.

In the neurotic world of *Peanuts*, Franklin is a rarity: he's relatively well-balanced. He is calm, levelheaded, and gets good grades. But he's under pressure, all right. His dad is in Vietnam, and the burden's on him at school to keep up the grades. He sometimes worries all night about tests and has so many after-school activities that he doesn't have time to play a simple game of marbles with Peppermint Patty. No one has an easy time of it in *Peanuts*.

JOINING THE GANG

Franklin first appears at the beach, when he rescues Charlie Brown's beach ball and they strike up a conversation about families and baseball while building sandcastles. Franklin then visits Charlie Brown's neighborhood. He meets Lucy offering psychiatric advice from a lemonade stand and Snoopy sitting on top of his doghouse in a flying helmet and goggles. Linus talks to him about the Great Pumpkin and Schroeder is counting the days until Beethoven's birthday. Even though he's a bit

► Franklin sits in front of Peppermint Patty at school and is center fielder on her baseball team.

PEANUTS

NOW, THERE YOU ARE, CHARLIE BROWN.. THERE'S A REAL SAND CASTLE!

◄ Franklin and Charlie Brown's friendship gets off to a good start. Franklin is one of the few characters who never says a mean word to Charlie Brown.

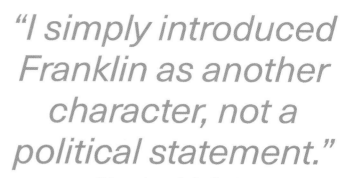

"I simply introduced Franklin as another character, not a political statement."
—Charles M. Schulz

▲ Although Franklin's first exposure to Charlie Brown's neighborhood leaves him "shook," he soon returns.

shaken up at first, he quickly becomes one of Charlie Brown's best friends. He likes discussing philosophy and theology with Charlie Brown and Linus. He also shares the wisdom of his grandfather, such as, "The secret to life is to be older than your lawn."

EXCHANGE OF LETTERS

Franklin entered the strip in the year that preacher and civil rights activist Martin Luther King Jr. was assassinated. Eleven days after the assassination, a former teacher from Southern California named Harriet Glickman wrote to Schulz, explaining that she wanted to help change the "vast sea of misunderstanding, fear, hate, and violence" that led to the assassination of Dr. King. She proposed that Schulz introduce a black character into the strip. Many years later, Schulz said, "I wasn't sure that I could do it, frankly. I don't know what it's like to grow up as a black kid." But he decided to give it a try and wrote to Ms. Glickman to tell her to be on the lookout at the end of July. After Franklin appeared, some newspapers threatened to drop the strip, but Schulz held firm. A reader wrote to complain, and Schulz said, "I didn't even answer him."

▲ This poseable porcelain figurine of Franklin was produced in 2000 by Hallmark in its Peanuts Gallery series.

▶ Franklin is sometimes at risk of burnout.

Anything Can Happen!

Schulz knew that, in a comic strip, anything can happen. Schroeder can play sonatas on a toy piano keyboard on which the black keys are merely painted on. Snoopy lives in a doghouse with its own TV aerial. Occasionally, Schulz liked to have the characters "break the fourth wall" and notice that they are cartoon characters. Aside from the strangeness of children talking like adults, *Peanuts* is all about the small, quietly odd moments that make up the everyday. But Schulz punctuates that with moments of pure surreality, often with Snoopy as the maestro of wild weirdness.

SELF-AWARENESS
For one strange moment, Schroeder becomes an actor in a comic strip called *Peanuts*.

MUSICAL SPRAY CAN
"Beethoven now comes in spray cans," announces Lucy to Schroeder in 1970.

GRAVITY BALLOONS

This strip from April 1975 illustrates a little-known law of speech balloons: two balloons together are too heavy to float.

IMPOSSIBLE BOUNCE

Lucy's bouncing ball defies the laws of physics in an early example of Schulz's deadpan surreality.

EYES OF INK

Lucy calls attention to the fact that Charlie Brown's eyes are dots of ink.

MIDAIR REVERSE

Snoopy can reverse in midair, even if he doesn't know how he does it!

A Love Not Shared

Lucy has her heart set on Schroeder, but Schroeder's heart is promised to Beethoven.

Lucy is used to being able to dominate others, running rings around Charlie Brown, Linus, and the rest. But Schroeder, the boy of her dreams, is immune to her ways. He is wrapped up in his music, dreaming only of being a great composer and asking for no adoration from anyone, especially not Lucy. Still, Lucy sits endlessly at the end of Schroeder's toy piano, talking to the top of his "cute" head while he hunches over the keys.

STRATEGIES FOR LOVE

Lucy tries to win over Schroeder by using many different strategies. Sometimes she tries to flatter his love of Beethoven and even helps celebrate his birthday, though she ruins it by singing "Happy Birthday, Karl Beethoven." When that doesn't work she tries to goad Schroeder by saying things like, "Beethoven never would have made it in Nashville!"

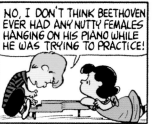

▲ Lucy knows that mentioning Beethoven is a sure way to get Schroeder's attention— but not his affection.

◄ Lucy props herself on the end of Schroeder's piano while Schroeder uses music to build a wall around himself.

"Each character has a weakness and Lucy's weakness is Schroeder."
—Charles M. Schulz

This just makes Schroeder angry and swipe his piano out from under her in utter contempt: "KLUNK!" Lucy then tries to ensnare Schroeder by imagining their future married life together. She tells him they will be so romantically poor that he will have to sell his piano for saucepans ("SAUCEPANS?!" Schroeder says in response). "After you learn to love me, sweetie," she says, "you'll appreciate my humor!"

LOVE RIVAL

It's hard when there are three in a relationship, and Lucy knows that Schroeder's piano is her love rival. She has tried getting rid of it, feeding it to the Kite-Eating Tree, and flinging it down a sewer. She has also tried to give up Schroeder. In 1971, she even returns all the gifts she was going to give him—"That didn't

even make sense!" she says. But it only lasts a week. For his part, Schroeder is clear that he barely tolerates Lucy, let alone loves her. But when she briefly moves away with her family in 1966, he actually finds that he misses her.

▶ Three's a crowd: the piano has to go! Schroeder later retrieves it from the storm drain: "Beethoven never had to put up with anything like this!"

▲ When Lucy moves away, Schroeder struggles with feelings he didn't even know he had. Unwittingly, Lucy has become his muse.

Collectible *Peanuts*

From the 1960s onward, Charlie Brown, Snoopy, and friends were everywhere, appearing on lunch boxes and sweatshirts, beloved by children and adults alike. From the creation of the first *Peanuts* products, Schulz was very much involved in the world of *Peanuts* outside the comics. "I wanted to make sure everything we did was right," he said. Where a lot of licensed merchandise was produced cheaply to cash in on a fad, Schulz made sure that anything with his characters on it was produced to a high quality. As *Peanuts* became an integral part of yearly rituals, from Valentine's Day and Halloween to Thanksgiving and Christmas, so too did its range of collectibles become part of people's lives—and Schulz's dedication to quality ensured *Peanuts* products would remain successful for many decades to come.

1 Charlie Brown shampoo, Avon (1970s) **2** Snoopy comb, Avon (1970s) **3** Bath bubbles, Avon (1970s) **4** Snoopy ("A Dog-On Funny Game") board game, Selchow & Righter (1960) **5** Simon Simple (1972) **6** Charlie Brown and Lucy sweatshirts, Determined Productions Inc. (1970s) **7** Lunch box and thermos, King Seeley Thermos (1974–1976) **8** Tableware set, unknown creator **9** Peanuts birthday plate, Determined Productions Inc. (1978) **10** Italian Bank Linus, Determined Productions Inc., (1969) **11** Megaphone, Chein (1970) **12** Jack-in-the-box, Determined Productions Inc. (1969) **13** Snoopy telephone, Determined Productions Inc. (1977) **14** Pop-up card, Hallmark (c1965) **15** Pinbacks (decorative buttons), Simon Simple (1960s–1970s)

On Screen and Stage

Snoopy has trod the boards and graced the silver screen in multiple TV and film animations.

In 1959, the *Peanuts* gang appeared as animated characters for the first time in TV advertisements for Ford automobiles. Although the animator, Bill Melendez, had worked previously at Disney and Warner Bros., he had found a way to avoid Disneyfying the *Peanuts* characters. Schulz said, "I told him, 'This is just a cartoon. Don't worry about making it so lifelike.'" The cartoonist and animator agreed to preserve the flat feel of the strip, allowing the characters to "flip" from one direction to another, rather than turning smoothly, as was more usual in animation.

FIRST TV SPECIAL

In 1963, independent television producer—and *Peanuts* fan—Lee Mendelson contacted Schulz with a pitch for a documentary about his work. The resulting half-hour film, *A Boy Named Charlie Brown*, featured another short animated sequence by Bill Melendez. Now, Mendelson received a call from the Coca-Cola company, which was looking to sponsor a *Peanuts* Christmas special. Thinking quickly, Mendelson claimed to have an outline ready—even

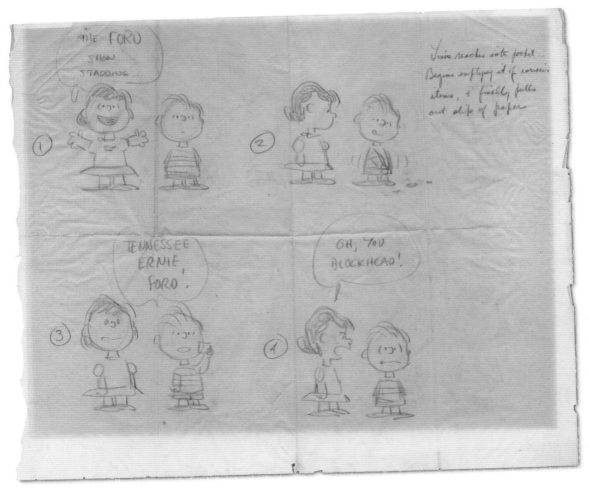

◀ Schulz drew this pencil sketch in around 1960 for an animated segment in *The Ford Show*, a variety program hosted by singer Tennessee Ernie Ford and sponsored by the Ford Motor Company.

◄ A limited-edition production cel, consisting of three cels taped together, from *A Boy Named Charlie Brown* shows the gang on the baseball mound.

though he hadn't even spoken to Schulz at this point! Luckily, Schulz loved the idea and *A Charlie Brown Christmas* was born. The creative team made several unusual and brave decisions: they used real young children's voices for the characters (some of whom were even too young to read), they avoided canned laughter, and they put Vince Guaraldi's cool, spare jazz trio on the soundtrack. The TV executives had misgivings about all these choices, as well as the relaxed pace of the show and its overtly religious message. However, when it aired on December 9, 1965, the show was a huge success, winning an Emmy award and becoming a cherished holiday tradition ever since.

▲ A reproduced animation cel showing the famous dancing scene from *A Charlie Brown Christmas.*

ENDURING PARTNERSHIP
The collaboration and friendship between Schulz, Melendez, and Mendelson endured until 2006, during which time more than 70 successful and award-winning TV animations were made, as well as four feature films. "All three of us have input," said Mendelson, "but it's 100 percent [Schulz's] creative control, and he has written most of the scripts."

PEANUTS ON STAGE
In 1967, *Peanuts* made the transition to the stage in a musical with actors playing Charlie Brown and the gang. *You're a Good Man, Charlie Brown* opened to rave reviews at Theatre 80 St. Marks in New York's East Village. It played to full houses for four years, followed by a spell on Broadway and tours around the United States and abroad. The play is now the most frequently produced musical in American theater history.

▲ The poster for the original stage production of *You're a Good Man, Charlie Brown* at Theatre 80 St. Marks, New York City, in 1967 and the Mayfair Theatre in London.

Snoopy's Home Ice

The Schulzes built and owned an indoor ice rink in Northern California.

▲ Schulz loved ice-skating since childhood. Even in his later years, he sponsored and played in an annual senior hockey tournament.

When Charles and (then-wife) Joyce Schulz moved from Minnesota to California in 1958, the one thing they missed was ice-skating—until they found a local ice rink in Santa Rosa. After this rink permanently closed, the Schulzes formed a grand plan: they would buy some land and build a new, bigger ice arena. They found a 6-acre (2.4-hectare) site on the edge of Santa Rosa, on Steele Lane, and Joyce led and supervised the project, deciding on an authentic Alpine theme. She hired the special-effects designer from the recent movie *Planet of the Apes* to create authentic-looking trees for the Swiss village. She sent a photographer to Switzerland to take landscape photographs, which were blown up to 125 feet (38 m) long and hung on the walls. She had chalet facades overlooking the ice rink, with window boxes and low-key lighting. There was a coffee shop, the Warm Puppy Café,

▲ The beautiful exterior styling of the ice arena re-creates the feel of a traditional Swiss Alpine village.

▲ Schulz's favorite seat in the Warm Puppy Café is still reserved for him. He sat here every day, chatting to whomever came by.

▲ Schulz–designed stained glass inside the lobby of Snoopy's Home Ice.

▲ Ice-skating Snoopy acts as name-dropping mouthpiece for Schulz.

where Schulz had a special seat by the door, as well as a studio for him and offices for staff. Schulz even designed *Peanuts*-themed stained-glass windows.

GRAND OPENING

The Redwood Empire Ice Arena, known locally as Snoopy's Home Ice, opened on April 28, 1969. The grand opening was a charity benefit ice show for 1,700 spectators, hosted by Schulz and featuring guest stars, including the San Francisco cast of *You're a Good Man, Charlie Brown*; the Vince Guaraldi Trio, known for the music in the *Peanuts* TV specials; and Olympic gold medalist Peggy Fleming—who inspired a crush in Schulz, which he transferred to Snoopy in the strip!

CONCERTS AND SKATING

The ice in the arena can be carpeted using a state-of-the-art system to allow rock concerts and performances—the 1970s and 1980s saw appearances by Liberace, Bill Cosby, Bob Newhart, Rod McKuen, Crystal Gayle, and David Letterman. The Ice Arena is still open for skating all year round, including, for a week each summer since 1975, Snoopy's Senior World Hockey Tournament, hosted by Jean Schulz, with participating teams from all over the world—and described by Charles Schulz as "a summer camp for adults."

▶ Snoopy skates across the ice in his winter cap and scarf on the cover of the program for the grand opening of the Redwood Empire Ice Arena on April 28, 1969. Guest appearances listed inside the program include Schulz's friend, Olympic champion figure skater Peggy Fleming.

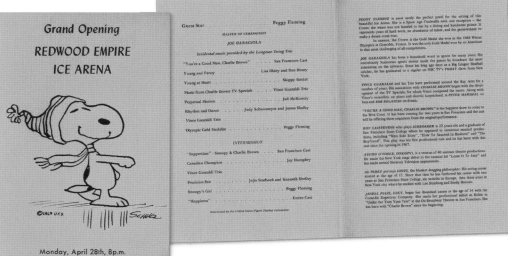

First Beagle on the Moon

We have liftoff! The bird is beginning to move. Snoopy's in space!

▲ You can tell that Snoopy is returning from the moon here, because he's facing the other way!

I n the 1960s, the race to get a man on the moon generated huge excitement. That excitement was raised a notch higher when, in March 1969, Snoopy emerged from his doghouse in a space suit and Flying Ace scarf! He then sat on his doghouse roof and blasted off into space, finally landing on the moon—which "looks like a dirty beach" apparently. Snoopy was just pleased that he had beaten everyone else—most importantly, the cat next door! Snoopy also beat Neil Armstrong by four months.

SILVER SNOOPY

Schulz's involvement with NASA had begun the previous year when he gave permission for Snoopy to be used as an award for spaceflight personnel whose efforts contributed to the success and safety of missions. Every one of these Silver Snoopy pins has been to space—carried by astronauts onboard round-trip spaceflights. NASA adopted Snoopy again

"I think having Snoopy go to the moon was the greatest triumph of all."
—Charles M. Schulz

◀ Charlie Brown is glad that Snoopy is going to the moon. It means he doesn't have to feed him that night!

◄ This Snoopy doll from 1969 depicts the beagle in a plastic bubble helmet, a red scarf, and blue rubber boots. His blue flight-safety box is attached to the suit with a hose.

◄ The design of the prestigious Silver Snoopy pin is based on a sketch drawn by Schulz.

in May 1969, with the launch of its Apollo 10 mission, a "dress rehearsal" for the mission that would land Neil Armstrong on the moon two months later. The spacecraft's lunar module was named *Snoopy* and its command module was named *Charlie Brown*. The *Snoopy* lunar module was dropped within 50,000 feet (15,000 m) of the moon's surface, and was then jettisoned into space—and is now thought to be in orbit around the sun! To this day, Snoopy remains a part of the space program at NASA. In 2019, NASA celebrated the 50th anniversary of the Apollo 10 mission and the Silver Snoopy partnership with school programs, a short feature film, and an exhibition at the Schulz Museum in California.

I'M ON THE MOON!

I DID IT! I'M THE FIRST BEAGLE ON THE MOON!

I BEAT THE RUSSIANS... I BEAT EVERYBODY.....

I EVEN BEAT THAT STUPID CAT WHO LIVES NEXT DOOR!

▲ The World Famous Astronaut becomes the first beagle on the moon.

► Snoopy and Charlie Brown figures decorate one of the stations in Mission Operations Control Room on the first day of the Apollo 10 mission in 1969.

"*I think that any humor which is really worthwhile is humor which comments upon some aspect of life.*"

—Charles M. Schulz

The World is changing

Reflecting the Times

COLD WAR PARANOIA
Reflecting the mood of widespread mistrust in Cold War America, in October 1956, Linus hopes that trick-or-treating won't arouse the suspicions of the FBI.

By the 1970s, Schulz's wry, gentle humor had made *Peanuts* the most widely read comic strip in American history. Schulz did not view *Peanuts* as a social commentary—"I never even think about it," he said. "I just draw what I think or what I hope will be funny things." Nevertheless, the strip always reflected what was going on in the world, and subtly—at times explicitly—engaged with serious national debates about such topics as fear of nuclear war, Cold War paranoia, and the Vietnam War.

VOTE FOR SNOOPY!
The 1968 presidential election campaign prompts Snoopy to stand as a candidate for "paw power." Unfortunately, his campaign "dwindles out"—and Richard Nixon wins.

PUPPY FARM PROTESTS

At a time when campus demonstrations over the military draft were being met with tear gas, Snoopy gets caught in the fray. At his old home, the Daisy Hill Puppy Farm, he tries to make a speech while a protest erupts over dogs being sent to Vietnam.

NUCLEAR FEAR

At a time of extensive nuclear testing in the United States and widespread fears about nuclear war, Linus mistakenly thinks that snowfall is a nuclear winter.

CLEAN UP AMERICA

In 1972, Snoopy lends his support to the Bureau of Land Management's anti-litter campaign in the lead-up to the bicentennial celebrations in the United States.

SUMMER OF LOVE

In July 1967, Snoopy encounters a "bird hippie" who complains that no one understands his generation. "No one understands my generation, either!" Snoopy comments.

Friend of Friends

Woodstock is Snoopy's wingman: best friend, confidant, secretary, protector, and New Year's Eve party thrower.

▲ Woodstock is Snoopy's best buddy. They sometimes argue with each other but always hug and make up.

Woodstock "came out of nowhere," Schulz said. "He was one of two undifferentiated little birds born in a nest on top of Snoopy's stomach." First seen in March 1966, one of these birds will become Snoopy's best friend, his "friend of friends"—though Schulz wouldn't name him until 1970. "I needed a name for him," Schulz averred. "And with the Woodstock festival being so prominent in the news, I said, 'Why not?'" He also knew a topical name would garner attention from "people that liked that kind of thing." At first, Woodstock was female, but Schulz decided to make him male: "It just happened. But that's what's good about a comic strip—you can just do it."

UNDER SNOOPY'S PROTECTION

Woodstock has always been a lousy flyer—more "flitter flutter" than actual flight—which at first irritates Snoopy. But Snoopy soon drafts Woodstock into a role as a mechanic on his Flying Ace missions and comes to sympathize when he crashes into things or flies upside down by mistake. Every fall, Woodstock heads south for the winter—or tries to, because he often goes the wrong way or gets lost. Once Snoopy even tried to walk him there! Snoopy doesn't know what kind of bird Woodstock is, despite trying to look him up in his *Guide to Birds* in 1980. "That's Woodstock's problem," said Schulz. "He doesn't know who he is." The main thing is that Snoopy understands him—

▶ Woodstock picks flowers for his long-lost mom, but ends up giving them to his "mother-substitute"—Snoopy!

▶ Woodstock became Snoopy's secretary when Snoopy was promoted to Head Beagle. He continues to do the job with a tiny typewriter—but not very well before coffee!

▶ In 1966, Snoopy finds that he's trapped on his doghouse until the two birds nesting on his chest have flown—one of the birds will turn out to be Woodstock.

▲ In 1972, Determined Productions Inc. made the first-ever Woodstock plush, manufactured in Japan.

"Woodstock knows that he is very small and inconsequential indeed. It's a problem we all have."
—Charles M. Schulz

after all, Woodstock only talks in little scratch marks, which Snoopy often translates for us. Schulz said, "I've held fast with Woodstock's means of communication, though it has been tempting at times to have him talk."

LIKE FAMILY
Snoopy and Woodstock soon become inseparable. They ice-skate and play football together, though poor Woodstock is too small to even kick the ball.

Snoopy even tolerates Woodstock's bird friends coming over on Saturday nights to party in his doghouse. But one thing Snoopy will never understand is why birds eat worms—it makes him feel "very, very, very, very, very sick!" For Woodstock, Snoopy is the only family he's got. He lost his grandfather (who escaped imprisonment in a cage and was never seen again), and his mother doesn't even visit on Mother's Day—though Woodstock often picks flowers for her, just in case.

▲ Woodstock's parties are hit-or-miss affairs—sometimes "boring," according to Snoopy, but at other times embarrassingly rowdy.

Too Cool for School

Here's Joe Cool—the quintessential college slacker hiding behind shades.

When Snoopy puts on a pair of sunglasses, he transforms into Joe Cool, college class-cutter and movie nerd—he's watched *Citizen Kane* 23 times! It's important to Joe Cool that he is seen to be doing nothing more than hanging out at the student union. Instead of taking classes, he plays Frisbee or watches movies—after all, "classes can ruin your grade average." He wants to be admired by female college students, though he admits to being scared to death of them. Despite, or because of, his cool arrogance, he is very much the aloof loner. Apparently, no one ever invites Joe Cool home for Thanksgiving. Nevertheless, his dorm (aka, his doghouse) gets all the "weirdos" and "strange ones"—like Linus, who moves in when Lucy kicks him out of his own house for breaking a crayon.

► In 1975, Joe Cool throws off his sweater and shades to keep up with the latest campus fad: streaking!

► What could be cooler than keeping your sunglasses on all the time and wearing a turtleneck sweater with your own name on it? Snoopy, *you've got this.*

◀ Joe Cool had his own range of cool merchandise, including this papier-mâché coin bank from 1977.

▲ Joe Cool with his world famous chopper in art created by the LoBianco Studio. Nick LoBianco has been creating art for *Peanuts* merchandise since the 1960s when Schulz approved him to ghost his style.

CAMPUS HUMOR

Joe Cool captured the irreverent spirit of campus humor that emerged in the 1970s with anarchic magazines such as *National Lampoon* and reached its apotheosis in 1978 with John Landis's frat-pack movie *Animal House*. Joe Cool even prefigured such icons of cool as Arthur "Fonzie" Fonzarelli from the TV show *Happy Days*, which first aired in 1974. The Fonz's catchphrase was "Sit on it!" while for Joe Cool it's "No way."

MORE JOE

Joe Cool isn't the only Joe that Snoopy becomes. He's also been Joe Motocross in leathers and bike helmet, Joe Preppy in houndstooth jacket and bow tie, and even Joe Grunge in 1993, looking like a reject from '90s rock band Guns N' Roses. When he says "merci, mon ami" to Charlie Brown, he's Joe French.

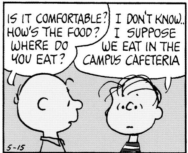

▲ Joe Cool just happens to have the same favorite food as Snoopy—pizza.

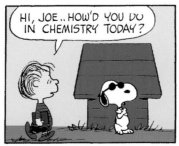

▲ Joe Cool hangs out at the student union for the first time in May 1971.

The School Building

Sally and her school building have more in common than either of them think.

Sally finds school hard, but who will listen? Not the principal, the PTA, or the board of education. So, she turns to the school building itself. At first, she kicks and threatens it, believing that it enjoys seeing innocent children being "tortured" inside. In response, it threatens to drop a brick on her. Once she's calmed down, Sally notices that its bricks are "cool." From this moment, Sally and the school building reach an understanding. The school begins to miss Sally on weekends. When Sally has to stay at home with an upset stomach, Charlie Brown has to inform the school building.

NERVOUS COLLAPSE

Even though Sally continues to appreciate the school—she even thinks it has cute steps—in January 1976, it starts to get depressed. It wanted to be an art institute or a music college instead of an elementary school, but now the principal complains that it doesn't have enough rooms and the building inspector criticizes it. Finally, the whole building collapses—"committed suicide," according to Sally. She has to go to Peppermint Patty's school while a new school

▲ Sally takes out her frustration on the school building itself for the first time in 1971. At this stage, it doesn't reveal that it has a consciousness.

▶ Sally sees "eye to brick" on certain things: a dislike of the school authorities and a dread of the start of term.

▲ By 1974, Sally and the school building have reached an understanding. Who knew that buildings need to be loved, too?

▶ The school building throws one of its own bricks at Lucy for calling it "stupid."

is being built. When it is, she warns it that the last one had a nervous breakdown and that this one should expect to be cursed and reviled. "I wanna go home," the poor building says. Nevertheless, they continue to chat for many more years and the building becomes a soothing place for Sally to rest her head, comforting her with words that Schulz's wife Jean used for him: "Poor sweet baby."

> ## "Going to our school is an education in itself, which is not to be confused with actually getting an education."
> —Sally

▶ Sally's beloved school collapses after being depressed for some time.

Great Friend

Marcie is a bookworm and intellectual who is unlikely best friends with a jock!

▲ Marcie wears a beret when she's in France with the World War I Flying Ace.

Marcie is studious, bookish, and wise. She gets great grades and prefers attending music concerts to playing sports. Yet she is best friends with D-minus student and sports fanatic Peppermint Patty. Schulz described them as an "unlikely pair," saying "they seem to have nothing in common, yet this is what makes their friendship so genuine."

DEVOTED FRIENDS
Marcie meets Peppermint Patty at summer camp in 1971. Patty thinks Marcie is "dorky" and "weird." But they quickly bond over a nighttime trip to the boys' camp across the lake. Marcie always calls Peppermint Patty "Sir," which Schulz ascribed to "admiration and misguided manners." She is devoted to Peppermint Patty and worries about Patty's difficulties with school—if she were her conscience, she says, she'd whip her into shape! Marcie joins in with football and baseball to show support for Peppermint Patty—and to show support for the cause of equality in sports for women. Marcie is exceptionally sweet-natured most of the time—but she can lose her temper. She stands up to bullies and won't back down from an argument with Peppermint Patty.

► Marcie is an excellent student and loves music and the arts. She takes organ lessons with Linus's teacher, Miss Othmar.

▶ Marcie goes on her first adventure with Peppermint Patty at summer camp in July 1971.

▲ When Charlie Brown is in the hospital, Marcie speaks for Peppermint Patty as well when she admits to loving him!

LOVE TRIANGLE

Marcie quickly intuits that Peppermint Patty is in love with Charlie Brown. For herself, she is always unfailingly admiring and respectful of "Charles," as she calls him, and even develops a small crush on him, too. Over the years, she and Peppermint Patty will vie for Charlie Brown's heart—which, of course, he's reserved for the unattainable Little Red-Haired Girl.

PRESSURE TO BE PERFECT

Marcie is the daughter of professional parents (her mother is a civil engineer). They expect her to get perfect grades and have already picked out a college for her. When the pressure gets to her, she crashes at Charlie Brown's house, which is a comfortingly "C-minus home," according to Sally. Marcie also loves to escape into fantasy. In 1974, she flies with Peppermint Patty on Snoopy's doghouse in the Powder Puff Derby (a real annual air race for women pilots, which Schulz's wife Jean flew in several times) and, later, plays the part of the "French lass" to Snoopy's Flying Ace. "Marcie is the smartest of the *Peanuts* gang," said Schulz, "but also the most naive."

▶ This limited-edition figurine from Dark Horse Deluxe was sculpted by Yoe! Studio artist Craig Yoe in the 2000s.

▲ Marcie acts as Peppermint Patty's conscience on school homework.

Little Brother

Rerun is Linus and Lucy's little brother. He loves dogs and underground comics.

I'M YOUR YOUNGER BROTHER, AND I DON'T SUCK MY THUMB OR CLING TO A BLANKET FOR SECURITY..

▲ Rerun prefers not to adopt Linus as a role model.

In May 1972, Lucy throws Linus out of the house just as their mother gives birth to her new baby brother. "But I just got rid of the old one!" Lucy shouts. "What irony," says Linus. "What swift retribution." For Lucy, who wanted to be an only child, or at least to have a sister, another brother is a "rerun"—like a TV show she's already seen. Thus, Rerun Van Pelt gets his name. He doesn't appear in person until March 1973, when he looks like a little Linus with scrawnier hair. Although Snoopy gives him a welcome lick only to discover that he tastes terrible, Lucy is surprisingly protective of him. She immediately finagles him a place on Charlie Brown's baseball team—after which the team wins its first-ever game! Unfortunately, the win is forfeited because of a gambling scandal: Rerun bet a nickel to win (Snoopy bet against!).

AT SCHOOL

In the 1980s, Rerun slips into the background, as Schulz admitted he had "run out of ideas" for him. However, in the 1990s, perhaps in response to Schulz himself becoming a grandfather, Rerun reenters the strip. He's finally old enough to go to kindergarten—though he spends the first week hiding under the bed. Once he gets there, he shows a talent for drawing underground comics, instead of watercolors of flowers.

► Rerun spends a lot of the 1970s on the back of his mother's bicycle, giving him plenty of time to think about people and life—and what would happen if they ran into a tree!

▲ Lucy adopts a sisterly attitude toward Rerun in his first appearance in the strip in March 1973.

▲ Rerun is into drawing underground comics. As Schulz said, "It's a shame cartooning is so rarely studied in schools."

"Rerun is more skeptical than his brother and always gets around Lucy where Linus gives in."
—Charles M. Schulz

LIKES AND DISLIKES

Rerun desperately wants a dog and his parents won't let him have one, so he constantly tries to borrow Snoopy— but any of Snoopy's eccentric siblings will do (except Spike). He also discovers he's very bad at basketball and marbles. Rerun knows he doesn't want Linus's habits of clutching a security blanket, sucking his thumb, and believing in the Great Pumpkin. Lucy makes it her personal mission to stop him from acquiring these habits. Rather than be associated with either of them, Rerun prefers to tell people he's an only child.

▶ In the 1990s, Rerun befriends a girl with pigtails at kindergarten. He is suspended for harassment after suggesting that they run away together: Schulz's dig at perceived political correctness.

Musical Notes

Schulz transcribed real classical scores from actual sheet music for strips featuring Schroeder's music. He admitted they could be "tedious" to draw, but he appreciated that "some readers enjoy trying to determine what it is that Schroeder is playing." Schroeder's music could sometimes fill the comic frame when he wanted to block out Lucy. By the 1970s, however, they started to have real physical presence, as characters bump into them, crumple them up, and sit or dance on them. Snoopy once took a handful of them and roasted them over a campfire. Schroeder once thought he must be dreaming—but we know better, don't we?

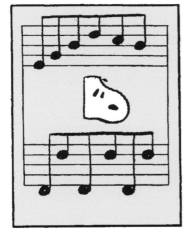
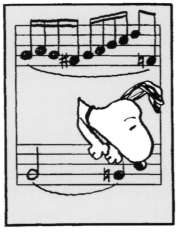

INTO THE MUSIC
As Schulz expands the range of his inspired surreality, Snoopy can climb on, behind, and through the music that Schroeder is playing.

WRINKLED SOUNDS

In response to being ignored by Schroeder, Lucy, quite reasonably, resorts to the impossible. Schroeder's response is equally surreal.

SNOOPY TO THE RESCUE

"I've been having the strangest dreams lately," Schroeder tells Lucy in October 1989: the notes he's playing have started to fall away. Luckily, Snoopy is practical in matters of the impossible.

MUSICAL KICK

Schroeder's notes push Woodstock away when he starts singing, as if in defense of their maker's refined ears.

Mr. Sack

Charlie Brown becomes Mr. Sack: camp president and hero (but only when his face is hidden).

▲ The other kids believe that Mr. Sack has great—almost mystical—powers.

In 1973, Schulz dreamed up "a neat little tale," of which, he said, "I was proud." Charlie Brown goes to summer camp with a paper bag on his head. He becomes the extraordinarily popular "Mr. Sack" and is elected president—but only while his true identity is concealed.

NEW IDENTITY

The story starts when a stressed-out Charlie Brown starts seeing baseballs everywhere: in the sky and on top of his ice-cream cone. He develops a rash that resembles baseball stitching on the back of his head. He goes camping with a paper bag over his head to hide the rash and is an instant hit with the other kids, who believe Mr. Sack has great powers. When he removes the sack, he becomes his old undistinguished self again.

BRIEF GLORY

"I don't pretend there is any great truth to this story," Schulz said, "or any marvelous moral." But camp, for Schulz, was always a link to his army experiences. Charles Schulz described himself in a Charlie Brown-ish way, as a "nothing person" when he went into the army, where he became a staff sergeant. "And I felt good about myself," he said, "and that lasted about eight minutes and then I went back to where I am now." Just like Charlie Brown!

▲ Charlie Brown has a restless night worrying about baseball. When the sun comes up, it's a baseball! He needs to visit Lucy's psychiatric booth.

▲ With a paper bag on his head, Charlie Brown finds out what it feels like to be highly respected by his peers.

▲ Would-be escaped criminal Charlie Brown is bowled over when he meets the Goose Eggs. Austin and Ruby display a deep lack of knowledge of older people.

The Goose Eggs

Charlie Brown finally finds a baseball team that looks up to him—literally. Meet the Goose Eggs.

The Goose Eggs is the name of a very young, very small baseball team that Charlie Brown manages for a short time in 1977. He first meets the two biggest members of this tiny team, Austin and Ruby, who accidentally knock him out with a stray baseball and then recruit him to be the manager of their team. They look up to him, figuratively and literally—tiny Leland is team catcher, although the mask covers his entire body! Minute Milo needs help with his batting—and just to be able to lift the bat.

ON THE RUN

The Goose Eggs live in a neighboring district and have no idea of Charlie Brown's poor reputation back home. Charlie Brown only meets them because he has run away from home after inflicting some well-deserved damage on the Kite-Eating Tree—he bit it! Now he fears the Environmental Protection Agency will throw him in jail. While managing the Goose Eggs he lives in a cardboard box, but Milo brings him breakfast: cold cereal, cupped in his own hands. He and Leland call Charlie Brown "Charles" and the whole team admires him. Even after failing to get them a game, Milo claims that he wants to be like Charlie Brown when he grows up. And Charlie Brown will take that.

▲ The Goose Eggs—Austin, Ruby, Leland, and Milo—get their name from the baseball term "goose egg," meaning zero, indicating that a team has scored no points at all.

The Beagle Scouts

Beagle Scout Snoopy leads the bird troops deep into the wilderness— beyond even the last supermarket cart!

n May 1974, Snoopy becomes a World Famous Beagle Scout—a pun on Eagle Scouts, the highest rank in the Boy Scouts of America. Thinking that the "N" on a compass stands for "Nowhere," he quickly gets lost in the suburban "wilderness." But soon he's leading Woodstock and his bird friends on nature hikes. They take with them only the necessities of life—which sometimes means golf clubs, sundials, surfboards, and pizza. Snoopy's Beagle Scout troop consists of Woodstock and his bird friends. Olivier is the most clueless bird scout: he brings the TV guide to a campout, thinks a whale might attack him at the top of a hill, and tries to hike while still in his sleeping bag. Harriet and Bill are the smartest. They are married in June 1983, with Snoopy acting as best beagle. Conrad completes all his tests and receives the "Beagle Scout" award, which makes him topple over when pinned to the side of his tiny hat. Fred, Roy, Wilson, and Raymond (who is distinguished by being a darker color than the others) appear only infrequently.

FOLLOW THE LEADER

The birds respect their beagle leader but don't always take scouting that seriously. Sometimes they prefer to go into town to disco all night, leaving Snoopy to "pork out on marshmallows." Sometimes they give into fear and flutter up to the safety of the brim of Snoopy's hiking hat.

► The scouts follow the example of the Beagle leader and sleep on top of their tents.

◄ The bird scout troop gathers on the brim of Snoopy's hat for safety from snakes, chicken hawks, and other potential enemies.

▲ The scout troop likes to bring marshmallows on hikes.

"Hiking, camping, and roasting marshmallows over an open fire can revive the writer's dampened spirit."

—Charles M. Schulz

▲ Snoopy only has a brief moment of indecision before allowing Harriet to join the troop—after all she's brought "angel food cake with seven-minute frosting."

► On a hike, the World Famous Beagle Scout gets completely lost and has to be rescued by a cookie-selling Girl Scout named Loretta.

◄ Four of the Beagle Scouts are featured on this 1999 camporee—or camping event—patch from Schulz's local Boy Scouts chapter in Santa Rosa, California.

► Snoopy knew that letting the scouts go into town to disco all night wasn't a good idea.

Spike

Spike is Snoopy's nonsmiling, desert-dwelling, cactus-adopting favorite brother.

▲ Spike goes into Needles to meet a "beautiful Hollywood-type girl" and instead meets kindhearted Naomi.

Snoopy's enigmatic older brother Spike lives by himself in the Mojave Desert outside Needles, California: the same "little sandy town" that Schulz lived in for two years with his parents when he was six. Spike was also the name of Schulz's childhood dog, the one with quirky habits, whom Schulz described as a "wild creature" who was "not completely tamed." When Spike visits for the first time in August 1975, Snoopy, the pampered suburban dog, is excited that his wild, root beer–drinking brother will punch the cat next door on the nose. However, when Spike actually arrives, he's "as thin as a promise," with moustache-like whiskers and a raggy fedora. After all, he's been living with coyotes (his job was to sweep out the den!).

LONER LIFE

Spike is the best man when Snoopy is engaged to be married, but he ends up running away with Snoopy's bride-to-be, who herself runs off with a coyote. For years afterward, Spike dreams

▶ Spike once sneaked into the Needles Chamber of Commerce building to plug in an extension cord for the lights on Joe Cactus. A statue of Spike stands at the building today.

► In between meetings of the Cactus Club, of which he is chairman, Spike seems to find plenty to do in the desert.

LIVING IN THE DESERT ISN'T ALL BAD...

THERE'S BEAUTIFUL SCENERY...

AND GOOD CONVERSATION..

HI, ROCK!

of meeting his dream beagle but must make do with rocks, tumbleweeds, and a saguaro cactus, which he calls Joe. Spike leads a lonely existence, but, as Schulz noted, "he seems to have a good time just the same." As Spike writes to Snoopy, "Life here on the desert is exciting. Last night the sun went down and this morning the sun came up. There's always something happening." He sometimes makes visits into Needles to play video games and in Hollywood he befriends Mickey Mouse, who gives him a pair of his shoes.

MYSTERIOUS PAST

Schulz summed up Spike: "There is about him … an air of mystery." Why did he choose the life of a loner, living in the California desert, far away from his family? All we know is what Spike revealed in 1994 to Joe Cactus: when he was young, he chased a rabbit—against his better instincts and egged on by friends—which ran across the road and got killed by a car. He came out to the desert so he couldn't hurt again. As for the rest, as Schulz says, "Our imagination takes over."

PEANUTS

SPIKE! GOOD GRIEF, YOU'RE AS THIN AS A PROMISE!

THIS IS THE MOST MISERABLE LOOKING DOG I'VE EVER SEEN!

I'M GONNA TAKE HIM HOME, AND FEED HIM!

POOR SPIKE

▲ On his first visit, Spike is adopted by Lucy, who makes it her mission to fatten him up.

► Spike has many one-sided conversations with Joe Cactus. Joe once envied Spike for being able to move, thinking "but I have to stand here for the rest of my life!"

DO YOU HAVE A COUSIN IN ARIZONA?

▲ A more-stylish-than-usual Spike in trench coat and stripy top, with whiskers made of black yarn, by Japanese toy company Tomy.

"Spike doesn't really smile much, since there's not much to smile about in the desert."
—Charles M. Schulz

Wrapped Snoopy House

Schulz liked to reference artists he admired in his strip, notably US artists Andrew Wyeth and Edward Hopper, turning Woodstock and pals into his famous painting *Nighthawks* in 1993. He also admired the Bulgarian-born, US-based artist Christo, maker of large-scale, site-specific artworks with his wife and artistic partner, Jeanne-Claude. Charles Schulz met Christo and Jeanne-Claude in 1974 when they were in Northern California working on the preparation for *Running Fence*, a 24-mile (39-km) fabric-and-steel fence that would extend across the hills of Sonoma and Marin Counties. In 1978, Schulz memorialized Christo in a strip in which Snoopy wonders what he'll do next: wrap his doghouse? Twenty-five years later, Christo did just that by creating *Wrapped Snoopy House*, a life-size doghouse wrapped in tarpaulin, polyethylene, and ropes. The artist presented it to Jean Schulz and it is now on permanent display at the Charles M. Schulz Museum.

ORIGINAL INSPIRATION

As well as *Running Fence*, Snoopy references Christo and Jeanne-Claude's *Valley Curtain*, a cloth stretched across a valley in the Rocky Mountains in 1971–1972, and *Wrapped Walk Ways*, nearly 3 miles (5 km) of fabric-covered footpaths in a park in Kansas City, Missouri.

"There is poetry in Christo's work and in Charles Schulz's work—the happy feeling of being alive—that is the common link."
—Jeanne-Claude

ARTISTIC GIFT
Christo's artwork was a recognition of the friendship and support Charles and Jean Schulz had shown in support of his *Running Fence* concept during the planning stages.

Mixed Doubles

Schulz falls in love with tennis during its boom in the 1970s and introduces some new sporty characters.

▲ One of the original illustrations Schulz did for the book *Tennis Love: A Parents' Guide to the Sport,* by Billie Jean King.

In 1972, Schulz's first marriage ended and he embarked on a new life with Elizabeth Jean ("Jeannie") Forsyth, whom he married in September 1973. Jean was a keen tennis player and Schulz, who had always played tennis, began to play more seriously, too. He took lessons and played in mixed doubles tennis tournaments. These new athletic pursuits found their way into the strip, along with some new characters.

SNOOPY AND MOLLY VOLLEY

Snoopy first appeared as the World Famous Tennis Player in 1970, taking lessons through a correspondence course and playing doubles with an improbable partner: the garage wall. In 1977, his new mixed doubles partner is gritty, determined Molly Volley. She learned to play not at fancy Wimbledon or Forest Hills, but on "dirty, bumpy, miserable courts," and she is single-minded about winning—even Snoopy seems a little afraid of her! "She is one tough cookie," said Schulz, "who embodies the widely held American belief that the only thing that matters is winning."

THE COMPETITION

Snoopy and Molly's competition is two spoiled brats: "Crybaby" Boobie and her partner, "Bad Call" Benny. "Crybaby" complains about everything

◀ Molly Volley has to contend with verbally abusive opponents like "Bad Call" Benny and a doubles partner who "blaps" the ball instead of "thonging" it!

▲ One of Charles M. Schulz's tennis rackets from the 1970s, with a personalized "Sparky" zipper case.

while her (unseen) mother sits in her car and honks the horn every time her daughter wins a point. "Bad Call" Benny seems to take his tennis style from famously argumentative player John McEnroe, calling everything out and insulting Molly. Faced with such unpleasant competition, Molly and Snoopy start to bond and even reach an understanding over chocolate-chip cookies. Unfortunately, Snoopy lets the cookies win in straight sets—he eats too many, gets sick, and loses the match.

TENNIS HERO

One of Schulz's heroes was tennis legend Billie Jean King, who founded the Women's Sports Foundation to promote female participation in sports and fight for gender equality on the field. The two became close friends and Schulz often mentioned her in the strip. They even collaborated on a book about teaching kids to play tennis—with the World Famous Tennis Player himself, Snoopy, demonstrating the concepts described by the former number-one women's tennis player.

▲ Peppermint Patty makes one of many references to Schulz's tennis hero and friend, Billie Jean King, in a strip from 1974.

► "Bad Call" Benny learns to be afraid of Molly Volley after she punched him for calling her "Fat Legs Volley."

► Molly Volley is no rich-kid dilettante— she is from the streets and is determined to win.

New Best Friend

▲ Sleeping out at camp, Eudora and Sally help each other manage their loneliness.

Eudora moves into the neighborhood and immediately causes a storm.

Schulz liked to borrow the names of people he knew for characters in the strip, although he stressed, "it's just the names I use—I would never take anyone's character." This would be a comfort to Eudora Welty, the Pulitzer-winning author whose name he gave to one of Sally's most featherbrained friends, introduced in 1978. Schulz met Welty several times when he donated money to an African-American college in her home state of Mississippi. Schulz said, "That was really one of the great moments of my whole life, just meeting someone like Eudora Welty." In turn, Welty spoke of her admiration for Schulz's writerly qualities: the way he had imagined the inside of Snoopy's doghouse but left it to the reader's imagination. "That's so good," Welty said. "A writer has to know all about the inside of a thing even if he is just going to show a little bit of it."

◀ Meeting Sally at camp for the first time in 1978, Eudora shows a cluelessness that surpasses even Sally's.

▶ Eudora is a good friend to Charlie Brown, whom she calls "Charles," and to Sally, who is a love rival for Linus. Snoopy also has a crush on Eudora, but she spurns him for his brother Spike!

NEW FRIEND

Sally meets Eudora at camp, and they become
instant friends. Sally isn't fazed that Eudora thinks
antelopes might eat her, falling stars might fall on
her, and that orientation is something to do with the
Orient. Sally, though not a fan of camp, finds herself
convincing Eudora that camp is fun—which she says
ruins her own miserable time. Eudora then transfers
to Sally's school from out of state (she doesn't know
where from). She wonders what a chocolate
sandwich would taste like with gravy on it and
attends school unaware that it's a Saturday.

BLANKET-GATE

Eudora charms the socks off Charlie Brown—
literally—and then charms the blanket off Linus with
her "cute smile." Snoopy attempts to charm Eudora
into giving the blanket back by disco dancing for
her, but he's too late—Eudora gave it away to the
dreaded cat next door. A terrible fight ensues, with
Linus and Snoopy mangled by the cat's sharp
claws. It takes Woodstock to calmly save the day.
After this tumultuous entrance, Eudora makes regular
appearances for the next nine years, playing on
Charlie Brown's football team, flirting with Snoopy's
brother Spike, and infuriating Sally by calling Linus
her "sweet babboo."

▲ Eudora first meets Linus, who loans her his blanket in
exchange for her cute smile, much to Sally's annoyance.

► As disco sweeps
the nation in 1978,
Snoopy gets in the
groove, attempting
to dazzle Eudora
into giving Linus's
blanket back.

Trust Issues

Three things in life are certain: death, taxes … and Charlie Brown's yearly humiliation as he tries to kick a football. Schulz thought of a new twist most falls for 47 years—from Lucy saying, "You have to learn to be trusting" to "Look at the innocence in my eyes." Depending on your point of view, Charlie Brown shows either heroic determination—the quality, Schulz believed, that distinguishes him from a true loser—or gargantuan gullibility. Lucy believes it is the latter, and she treats the ritual as a yearly lesson in human nature for Charlie Brown: not to be so trusting. "What you have learned here today, Charlie Brown," she says in 1968, "will be of immeasurable value to you for many years to come." According to Schulz, "Here's a young boy who is too innocent, too naive, and too trusting, dealing with somebody who is just too sure of herself. And he is incapable of combating her shrewdness."

LIFE LESSON

Lucy gives Charlie Brown a lesson in one of what she perceives to be his gender's failings.

FIRST FALL

The first time Lucy holds the football, in 1952,
she really holds it. The result is the same.

CHILDHOOD RITUAL

A two-year-old Schulz goes to kick a football held
by his cousin in 1925. Schulz remembered being
unable to resist the temptation of pulling away the
football as a child. "We all did it; we all fell for it."

> "*Charlie Brown, because
> of the qualities of his
> personality, simply
> cannot compete on the
> same level with Lucy.*"
> —Charles M. Schulz

RERUN TAKES OVER

The very last football gag strip, in 1999, features Rerun holding the
ball as a proxy for Lucy and ends on a cliff-hanger. Like Schrödinger's
famous alive/dead cat, we will never know—did he or didn't he?

Speaking Out!

▲ In 1979, Peppermint Patty is intent on recruiting Charlie Brown to the cause—although he's never had a problem with girls playing on the baseball team.

Schulz's strongly realized, nonstereotypical female characters always speak their minds.

Since the start of the strip in 1950, Schulz had resisted the then-entrenched notions of gender norms. The *Peanuts* world was not only dominated by children, but dominated by strong, outspoken female characters. Early characters such as Violet and Patty were absolutely not "all sugar and spice"—just as the boys defied gender stereotyping in their own way, too. In *Peanuts*, characters are allowed to be individuals, with their character flaws and insecurities laid bare.

LUCY

With the introduction of strong-willed Lucy, Schulz created one of the strongest female characters seen in mainstream American culture. She is both self-assured and cutting, a businesswoman (offering advice for five cents) and potential president, but not immune to moments of doubt and insecurity, too. Lucy often self-identified as a feminist and a supporter of what was

► Thibault tells Marcie that girls shouldn't be allowed to play baseball and should learn their proper place—and suffers the consequences.

▲ Lucy not only proves the boys wrong by belting out the home run they bet she couldn't hit, she also puts principles before passion by refusing Schroeder's kiss.

then called "women's lib." It's in the name of women's lib that she refuses a much-longed-for kiss from Schroeder: she won it in a bet, but since she knows it wouldn't be willingly given, she passes.

PEPPERMINT PATTY

Peppermint Patty is the strip's true individualist. She's better at sports than all her male friends, wears her hair short, with a striped T-shirt and shorts, shunning the dresses the other girls wore regularly. She's the only character who wears open-toed sandals— and will fight the school dress code for her right to wear them. She becomes a spokesperson for Schulz's support of Title IX, which banned gender discrimination in federal educational activities or programs. Marcie supports the cause, though she'd rather be playing her electric organ than doing sports. But when it comes to out-and-out male chauvinists like Thibault, Marcie, too, speaks out.

"Is Lucy a feminist or a jerk? Can't she be both?"
—Jean Schulz

► Lucy for President campaign button—"Or else!" She also has ambitions to be queen!

► Peppermint Patty's extensive listing of female players shows Schulz as a keen supporter of women's sports.

Cartoon Sounds

Peanuts is known for its quiet, conversational focus and its focus on small incidents. But equally characteristic is its range of distinctive cartoon sounds, from slapstick effects like "Pow!" and "Wump!" to the unique representation of Woodstock's voice—a series of little scratch marks—and the "Aaugh!" that almost all characters emit when reaching a pitch of frustration. Schulz was also a master of subtle sounds such as Charlie Brown's (and everyone's) resigned "Sigh!" Another distinctive exclamation is "Bleah!" which captures the feeling of, well, bleah—there's no better word for it. Darkest of all is the messy scribble, devoid of all sound, expressing the blackest of moods.

> ## "I'm the fastest letterer in the West. Not doing your own lettering is like Arnold Palmer having someone else hit his 9-irons for him."
>
> —Charles M. Schulz

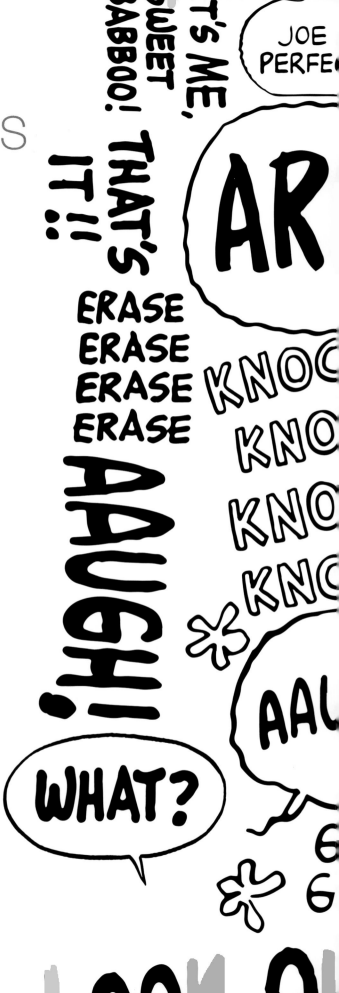

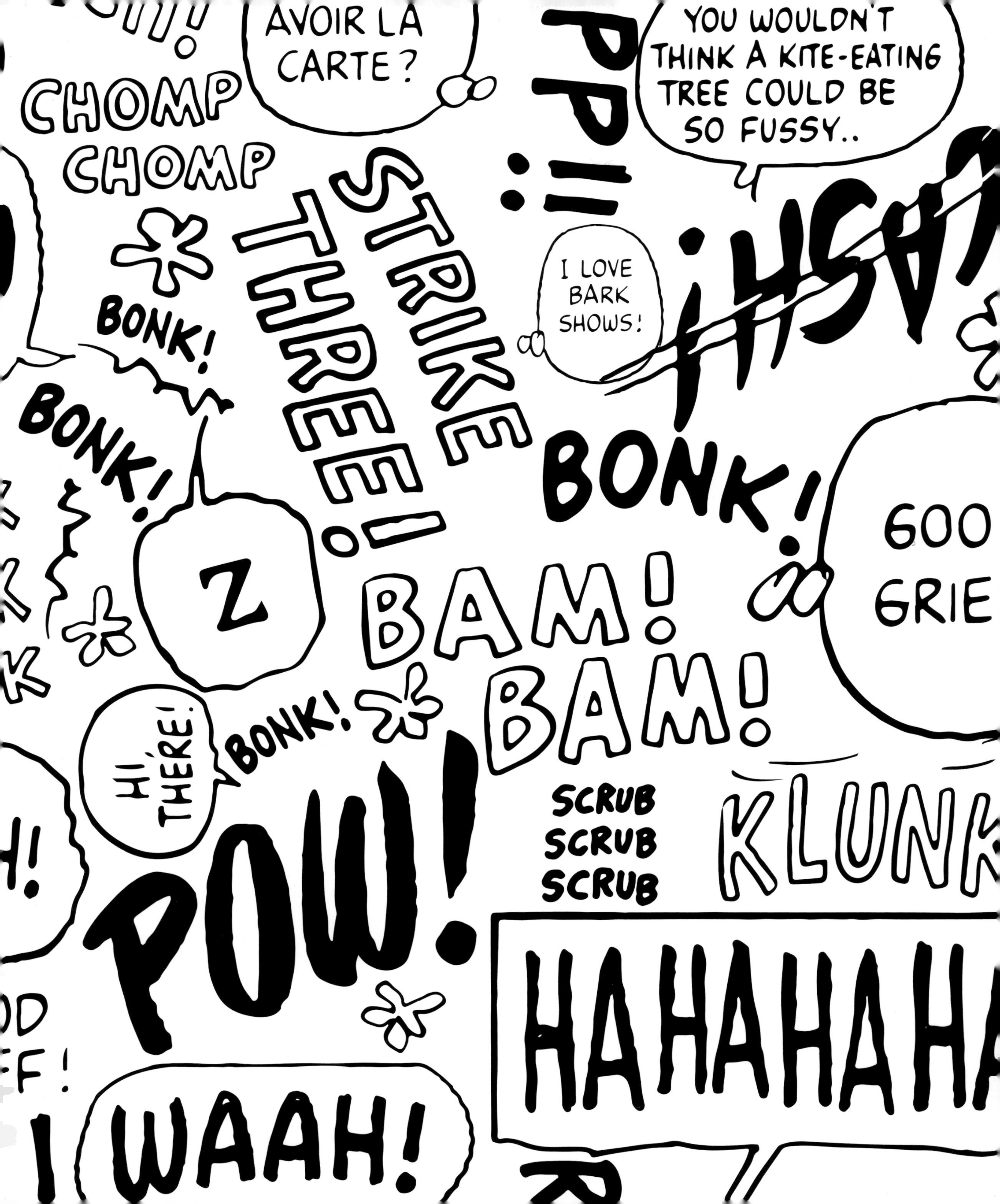

AVOIR LA CARTE?
CHOMP CHOMP
YOU WOULDN'T THINK A KITE-EATING TREE COULD BE SO FUSSY..
STRIKE THREE!
I LOVE BARK SHOWS!
BONK!
BONK!
BONK!
Z
BAM! BAM!
HI, THERE!
BONK!
POW!
SCRUB SCRUB SCRUB
WAAH!

"To take a blank piece of paper and continue drawing with the same pen and materials as when I started the strip in 1950 is a privilege. To draw characters that people love and worry about is extremely satisfying."

—Charles M. Schulz

Life Goes On

◀ Cormac practices his sweet talk on Marcie, who remains unimpressed.

Passing Acquaintances

At school and summer camp, the gang are a magnet for oddballs, hangers-on, and pushy know-it-alls.

Many characters enter the strip and play minor but engaging roles. The improbably named Harold Angel is a boy in Sally's school. He intends to comfort Sally after she flubs her only line in the school nativity play: her line is "Hark!" but she accidentally says "hockey stick." The plot thickens when Harold asks Sally to the movies but, according to Sally, her "boyfriend" Linus wouldn't want her to go—although his exact words are, "I'm not your sweet babboo and I wouldn't care if you went to Siberia."

SCHOOL CRUSHES

Linus has relationship problems of his own. At school, he tries to win the attention of a girl called Lydia, who he thinks is cute. Unfortunately, she thinks he's too old for her by a whole two months. Then there's Tapioca Pudding, whose dad, Joe Pudding, is in licensing and has convinced his daughter that, with her name, hair, and smile, they can make millions. She's going to be on lunch boxes, cards, T-shirts, TV—"everything." She goes on a date with Linus, causing a jealous Sally to remark that her face

would look "a lot better on a dog dish." Finally, Tapioca gets a World Famous agent by the name of Snoopy, who books her for the 1984 Olympic Games in Los Angeles—in 1986!

▶ Charlie Brown and Linus assume Harold Angel exists only in Sally's muddled mind—until he turns up on the doorstep.

"I want to remind adults of the pressures children are always being put under."
—Charles M. Schulz

SUMMER PALS

At summer camp, Charlie Brown gives a swimming lesson to a naive but self-confident little kid called Cormac, who then tries to smooth-talk Marcie. Later, Cormac sits behind Sally in school and tries to smooth-talk her, too. Back home, in 1993, Charlie Brown's baseball team finally wins a game, and, afterward, the pitcher on the opposing team tells him that he "ruined her life." Royanne Hobbs is the great-great granddaughter of Roy Hobbs, though she doesn't seem to realize that he is a fictional baseball player in a 1952 novel *The Natural* by Bernard Malamud.

BIBLE SCHOOL

Schulz's gentle Christianity has always been an understated theme in the strip, with Linus often the mouthpiece for Biblical quotation. In 1991, he and Sally open a Bible school. It surprises Sally that there are people who know less than she does, but Larry, despite being a minister's son, is one of them. He thinks the Great Gatsby is a character in the Old Testament. He also develops a crush on her.

▲ Ethan wants to become a newspaper columnist because he has strong opinions—about Charlie Brown's shirt.

▲ Tapioca Pudding is brought up in a family where a licensing deal is more important than ice cream.

► Royanne sells Lucy a bat that "was used by Roy Hobbs"—who Charlie Brown informs her is a fictional character.

Snoopy's Family

Snoopy is the most notable beagle in a large litter of eccentrics, loners, and individualists.

▲ The Flying Ace has a family reunion in World War I France with Red Cross nurse Belle and infantryman Spike.

Snoopy is cagey—or forgetful—about his family. Initially, he believes he's an only dog, then he remembers, incorrectly, that he has two brothers and three sisters, and afterward thinks he is one of a litter of seven. It turns out he is one of eight siblings, though only six of them are seen in the strip, with two more appearing in TV animations.

SPIKE AND BELLE

The first to appear, in 1975, is desert-dwelling Spike, followed by Snoopy's sister Belle a year later. Snoopy catches up with her in Kansas City, when he is en route to Wimbledon to play tennis. Belle was married to a "worthless hound" who left her and she has a teenage son, who is tall and thin like "the Pink Panther." In 1981, Belle turns up in Snoopy's World War I adventures as a Red Cross nurse, along with Spike who is in the infantry.

MARBLES, OLAF, AND ANDY

In 1982, Snoopy gets a letter from another brother, Marbles. Snoopy doesn't remember much about him except that he was the smart one. He has distinctive markings and wears jogging shoes. Snoopy takes him on a World War I flying mission in his Sopwith Camel—which scares off rational-minded Marbles so completely that he is never seen again. Then, in 1989, an ugly dog contest is held in the neighborhood. After initially proposing that Spike enter, Snoopy decides that his brother Olaf—"ugly Olaf"— would have the best chance of winning. He's right, and Snoopy regains contact with

► Belle is "just as beautiful as ever" according to Snoopy. But her son is apparently a "disappointment."

   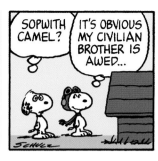

▶ Marbles comments that Snoopy was "always the quiet one" when he takes him on a flying mission.

another sibling: the "roly-poly" one. Finally, in 1994, Snoopy's "fuzzy" brother Andy turns up when Snoopy is admitted to the hospital with pneumonia. Schulz named Andy for his and Jean's own dog, a fox terrier for whom Schulz said he had a "fanatical love." After that, Andy is always paired with Olaf, and they wander around looking for Spike, working as farmhands and sled dogs, and generally searching for a purpose. Schulz was undoubtedly fond of Spike, but he came to believe that the introduction of Snoopy's other siblings may have been a mistake. He said, "it destroyed the relationship that Snoopy has with the kids, which is a very strange relationship."

▶ Belle became a popular character in licensed products. This 1980s Belle doll, known as a Collector Doll, has poseable joints and carries a yellow Walkman.

▲ Snoopy's dad makes his one appearance in the strip on June 18, 1989. He is retired and living in Florida when he receives a Father's Day card.

"Just saying 'beagle' makes me smile."
—Charles M. Schulz

▲ Snoopy's mother makes her single appearance in a Flying Ace flashback on July 26, 1996. Wearing a fur hat, she is onboard a World War I troopship to visit infantry-dog Spike, who is ill.

▲ Snoopy shares his hospital lunch with brothers Andy, Spike, and Olaf.

Looking for Answers

Charles Schulz and the *Peanuts* gang consider life's mysteries in their own inimitable ways.

▲ Robert L. Short's book, *The Gospel According to Peanuts*, published in 1965, used Schulz's characters to illustrate lectures on Christianity. It sold over 10 million copies.

In 1986, Sally invents a simple but effective philosophical framework for dealing with life: "Who cares?" She follows this up with many new philosophies, from "Why me?" and "How should I know?" to "Life goes on" and "Where will it all end?" (not to mention "We'll always have Minneapolis"). Though not especially interested in enlightenment (unless the bulb in her bedside lamp needs changing!), Sally is nevertheless one in a long line of *Peanuts* philosophers: Charlie Brown, Linus, Lucy, Schroeder, and others have all propped their arms on the neighborhood wall and reflected on the meaning—or meaninglessness—of existence.

RELUCTANT INTELLECTUAL
In interviews, Schulz downplayed his intellectual side, camouflaging it with self-deprecating humor, saying, "I never thought of myself as having any kind of philosophical approach." He was once described as "the youngest existentialist," though his response was typical: "What is existentialism?"

◀ At the end of the 1960s, Lucy seeks certainty in an increasingly questionable world, whereas Linus mocks easy simplicities.

◄ Linus experiences a Zen moment of existential insight.

In fact, he had read about leading French existential writer Jean-Paul Sartre in the *New York Times* and agreed with his view that "it was very difficult just to be a human being." Charlie Brown is proof of that! Schulz acknowledged that his strip gave him "the opportunity to express many of my own thoughts about life and people." His characters use the Gospel, which they can cite extensively, to frame their lives, while struggling with dark thoughts of worry and a prevailing sense of doubt. Notably, Schulz insisted—against his producer's advice—that one whole minute of the primetime TV special *A Charlie Brown Christmas* would feature Linus reciting the Gospel of Luke in search of the true, noncommercial meaning of Christmas. Schulz's instincts were proved right when TV audiences and critics were charmed and moved.

SCHULZ'S FAITH

Schulz embraced Christianity at the end of World War II, finding solace and companionship in it after his eventual return to civilian life. Like Linus, Schulz was a thoughtful scholar of the Bible, and he taught at Sunday school in Minnesota and California. He was no dogmatic believer, though, and chose not to impose his faith on his own children. As he grew older, his faith remained quietly reverent but became increasingly humanistic. He said, "I think the only pure worship of God is by loving one another."

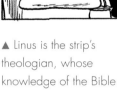

▲ Linus is the strip's theologian, whose knowledge of the Bible matched Schulz's own.

◄ Snoopy captures the emerging spirit of the 1960s in 1966.

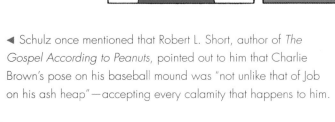

◄ Schulz once mentioned that Robert L. Short, author of *The Gospel According to Peanuts*, pointed out to him that Charlie Brown's pose on his baseball mound was "not unlike that of Job on his ash heap"—accepting every calamity that happens to him.

Working in Pencil and Ink

Schulz is known for the confidence of his penwork and his ability to produce final inked drawings without initial sketching. But he also made many sketches on paper. "A person has to start someplace," he said, "and I have found that this is my best way." He would sketch as a warm-up exercise on a Monday, and felt that many of his "most spontaneous ideas come from doodling in this manner." He discarded or gave away many of these sketches.

In the mid-1990s to early 2000s, Schulz's secretary at Creative Associates, Edna Poehner, retrieved many of his sketches from the garbage can. These rough drawings, often on letterhead, low-quality newsprint, or lined yellow legal paper, provide insights into Schulz's creative processes.

OUT TO SEA
In this preliminary sketch from 1976, Schulz drew in pencil on white notepaper.

SNOOPY PROFILE
In this portrait of Snoopy, from a "chalk talk" in the 1960s, Schulz used charcoal on a sheet of newsprint.

BASEBALL RAIN

Schulz took pride in being able to render rain effectively, saying, "Rain is fun to draw. I pride myself on being able to make nice strokes with the point of the pen." This drawing was one of 61 original drawings Schulz made for the book *Things I've Had to Learn Over and Over and Over*, published in 1984.

"CHALK-TALK" KITE

This sketch from the late 1950s shows Charlie Brown shaking his fist at a kite that has fallen into a trash can.

PATTY'S COURSES

Schulz often inked the text and final panel before completing the rest of the strip, as seen in this incomplete strip dating from 1974.

Charlie Brown's Love Life

Nothing quite works out for Charlie Brown and the girls in his life.

Charlie Brown's great love, the Little Red-Haired Girl, would always remain his unattainable ideal. But over the years, Charlie Brown meets several girls who are drawn to him. He even has a girlfriend for many years in the 1990s, though, as Schulz would say, "nothing seems to work out right" for good ol' Charlie Brown.

PEGGY JEAN

In 1990, Charlie Brown meets a girl called Peggy Jean, who becomes his girlfriend. Charlie Brown first speaks to her in the lunch line at summer camp. Unfortunately, he has an attack of nerves and tells her he's called "Brownie Charles." Afraid to correct her, he just goes with it and even comes to find it endearing. The first big test of their relationship is nearly the end of it:

▶ Charlie Brown meets his soon-to-be longtime girlfriend Peggy Jean: her name seems to combine Jean, Schulz's wife, with Peggy Fleming, the Olympic skater on whom he had a crush.

Peggy Jean holds a football for Charlie Brown to kick. Thoughts of Lucy in his head, he dithers about kicking it until she gives up and goes away, believing he doesn't trust her. Ultimately, they kiss and make up, and it must be love because Charlie Brown sells his entire comic

◀ One of the most heartbreaking moments in the strip is when Peppermint Patty finally meets the Little Red-Haired Girl that "Chuck is always talking about."

► Marcie and Peppermint Patty both have unrequited crushes on Charlie Brown.

book collection to buy Peggy Jean a special pair of gloves as a gift. In the end, Peggy Jean moves away and even gets a new boyfriend, leaving Charlie Brown heartbroken.

DANCE PARTNERS

In 1995, Charlie Brown is taking dance lessons when a girl named Emily unexpectedly asks him to dance. But when he goes back, she's nowhere to be seen, so he doubts that she ever existed. Not long after, he gets a phone call: it's Emily, inviting him to the Sweetheart Ball. He hadn't imagined her after all! But again, nothing works out right. He is dancing with Emily at the ball when Snoopy arrives and, since dogs aren't allowed, they both get kicked out. Charlie Brown and Emily share one more dance together in 1999 but then are parted … for Charlie Brown, love will always be just out of reach.

LOVE RIVALS

Closer to home, two of Charlie Brown's best friends are in love with him, though he never seems to realize it. Peppermint Patty took a few years to fall for him, though Marcie liked him right away—and could see immediately how Peppermint Patty felt, despite Peppermint Patty barely admitting it to herself, let alone to others. Marcie tries many times to tell Charlie Brown how she feels about him, but Peppermint Patty's crush is more complicated—rather than admitting that it is she who likes him, she pretends that it's he who likes her. A heartbreaking moment comes when Peppermint Patty meets the Little Red-Haired Girl at camp in 1972 and bursts into tears, thinking she is less attractive. Poor Charlie Brown just can't understand why anyone *would* like him.

▲ Peppermint Patty finds it hard to accept that she has feelings for Charlie Brown. Her reverse psychology just makes things more complicated!

► Emily makes her first appearance at Charlie Brown's dance class but vanishes afterward.

1980s and 1990s Memorabilia

1

Snoopy embraced the 1980s in a big way. His love of the 1983 movie *Flashdance* led to an animated special in 1984, *It's Flashbeagle, Charlie Brown*, and an accompanying soundtrack album, released by Disneyland Records's Charlie Brown Records label. Snoopy also got in on video-gaming action with games like Nintendo's Game & Watch Table Top Snoopy game from 1984, where Snoopy has to bash the musical notes coming from Schroeder's piano with a hammer! Meanwhile, the 1990s saw such items as Pez dispensers for each of the gang and ranges of soft toys and figurines from Applause. The true classic of the period, however, must be Hasbro's Snoopy Sno-Cone Machine, which first hit shelves in 1979 and was a top-seller right through the 1980s and '90s. It is still manufactured today by Cra-Z-Art—in fact, *Time* magazine named it one of the most influential toys of all time.

2

3

4

5

1 *Peanuts* PEZ Dispensers, PEZ Candy Inc. (c.1993)   **2** Snoopy Lying on Top of a Hotdog, Determined Productions Inc. (1982)   **3** Boy Snoopy, Determined Productions Inc. (1984)   **4** Peppermint Patty Doll, Determined Productions Inc. (1990)   **5** Set of five McDonald's glasses from the "Camp Snoopy Collection," McDonald's (1983)   **6** Battery Operated Schroeder Piano, International Trading Technology (1993)   **7** Snoopy in US mail truck, Aviva Inc. (1984)   **8** *Flashbeagle* LP album, Vista Records (1984)   **9** Snoopy Sno-Cone Machine, Playskool (c.1985)   **10** Daisy Hill Puppies figurines, Determined Productions Inc. (c.1990)   **11** Mr. T's Little Buddy, Mr. S; Determined Productions Inc. (1984)   **12** Peanuts Gang Music Box, Schmid Bros. Inc., (1984)   **13** Game & Watch Table Top Snoopy, Nintendo (1983)

To Remember

Schulz had served in World War II and had never forgotten the experience. He greatly admired the soldiers who had given so much during the D-Day landings on the Normandy coast in June 1944, and he wanted to call Americans at the end of the 20th century to remembrance. On Sunday, June 6, 1993, Schulz's first commemorative D-Day strip was published. A year later, on the 50th anniversary of D-Day, Snoopy spent a week playing out the Normandy Invasion, and Schulz continued the tradition most years that decade, receiving many letters from grateful veterans and their families. In 1997, Schulz donated a million dollars to help build the National D-Day Memorial in Bedford, Virginia, and with his wife Jean headed the fundraising committee. Sadly, he did not live to see the memorial's opening in 2001, nor that of the World War II Memorial in Washington, D.C.

JUNE 6, 1944, "TO REMEMBER"

D-DAY
A Nazi bunker; an Allied troop ship; and, in the final panel, GI Snoopy, crawling onto the beach—the images in the first D-Day commemorative strip from 1993.

© 1998 United Feature Syndicate, Inc.

5-31

JUNE 6, 1944 - TO REMEMBER -

PRESIDENT'S ADDRESS

In 1998, Schulz placed Snoopy into a colorized photograph of General Eisenhower addressing the troops of the 101st Airborne Division just before they parachuted into France. Schulz received many letters from those in the picture, and he signed copies for them and their families.

GARDEN GI SNOOPY

Snoopy's D-Day antics in the backyard in 1994 cause complaints from the neighbors.

"It's easy for us, as generations come and go, to forget what other generations did."
—Charles M. Schulz

CHEERS TO BILL

Since 1969, Schulz had memorialized fellow cartoonist Bill Mauldin on Veterans Day. Mauldin's cartoons depicting bedraggled infantry soldiers Willie and Joe had been popular among soldiers during the war.

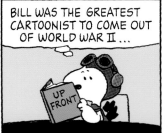

Endings

In November 1999, Schulz suffered several small strokes and was rushed to the hospital, where he was found to have stage IV colon cancer. Undergoing chemotherapy and with his health fragile, on December 14, 1999, Schulz announced his retirement in a letter to his hundreds of millions of fans around the world. In response, he made front-page news and was inundated with letters and bouquets from well-wishers. As his health deteriorated, he released a retirement strip, which was used again on February 13, 2000, in the final Sunday strip, which showed some of the cartoon's most beloved visuals: the football trick, Snoopy as the Flying Ace, Lucy's psychiatric booth, and Snoopy stealing Linus's blanket. This final *Peanuts* strip appeared just hours after Schulz passed away peacefully in his sleep at home. In respect of his wishes, no other cartoonist has continued the strip.

WITH ADMIRATION
In May 2000, cartoonists of more than 100 comic strips honored Schulz's passing by incorporating his characters into their strips. Editorial cartoonist Tim Menees's heartfelt tribute appeared in the *Pittsburgh Post-Gazette*.

FAREWELL WORDS
The final strip borrowed its title panels from an earlier strip that appeared in November 1999. Schulz chose some of the small moments that had made him laugh over the years, including Sally leaning over the arm of Charlie Brown's chair and a baseball bouncing off Lucy's head with a BONK!

FRIENDSHIP GIFT
Pulitzer Prize–winning cartoonist Mike Luckovich hand-colored his 1999 tribute panel as a gift for Schulz in January 2000.

LIFE WITHOUT *PEANUTS*
Cathy Guisewite, who drew the strip *Cathy* and knew Schulz for 20 years before his death, marked his retirement with this strip, published in January 2000.

SPARKY POWER
Marvel Comics supremo Stan Lee pays tribute to Schulz in 1999 with Spider-Man meeting Snoopy.

HOW WE LOVE HIM
Marking Schulz's retirement in January 2000, Patrick McDonnell, creator of one of Schulz's favorite daily strips, drew and hand-colored this tribute strip for "the greatest of 'em all," Sparky.

JUST GRIEF
Original cartoon by Steve Kelley, published in February 2000 in the *San Diego Union-Tribune*.

GAME OVER
Editorial cartoonist Mike Thompson's tribute appeared in the *Detroit Free Press* in 1999.

"The most wonderful part of the business is knowing that you are reaching people and communicating with them."
—Charles M. Schulz

Peanuts Everywhere!

Meet Snoopy

Outside of the pages of the comic, *Peanuts* fans can interact with Snoopy, Charlie Brown, and the gang at the annual Macy's Thanksgiving Day Parade in New York City and at theme parks and events across North America and beyond. Camp Snoopy at Knott's Berry Farm in Buena Park, California, was the first theme park, opening in 1983. It was followed by Camp Snoopy at the Mall of America in Bloomington, Minnesota, in 1992, which became the largest indoor amusement park in the Unites States. Several more Camp Snoopy parks opened across North America and were upgraded and renamed Planet Snoopy in the early 2010s. *Peanuts*-themed parks have also opened in Asia, including a play area called Snoopy's World in a mall in Hong Kong, Snoopy Garden in a mall in Beijing, and Snoopy Studios in the Universal Studios theme park in Osaka.

TAKING TO THE SKIES
The Macy's Thanksgiving Day Parade in New York City has featured *Peanuts* characters as huge helium-filled balloons since 1968. This concept plan drawing of Charlie Brown with his football (*below*) visualized the 2002 parade.

SPECIAL STATUS

Charles "Sparky" Schulz was made an honorary ranger at Camp Snoopy in 1983—Snoopy's paw print makes it official!

SITE VISIT

Charles Schulz visits Camp Snoopy prior to its opening in 1983.

SNOOPY'S WORLD

Opened in 2000 in Hong Kong, visitors to Snoopy's World enter via a huge doghouse with an approximately 11-foot- (3-m-) tall Snoopy statue on top. Then you can take a canal ride with Charlie Brown and his friends, play in the baseball-themed playground, and even get married in Snoopy's Community Hall!

CITYWIDE TRIBUTE

Peanuts on Parade was an exhibition of more than 100 *Peanuts* statues decorated by various artists, which ran in Schulz's hometown of St. Paul, Minnesota, from 2000 to 2004. After that, it moved to Schulz's California hometown of Santa Rosa, where it ran until 2010.

Schulz on Display

The idea of a museum devoted to Schulz's work was first discussed in the 1990s. At that time, Schulz was busy on the strip itself and didn't warm to the idea of becoming a museum piece himself! However, his wife Jean, along with cartoon historian Mark Cohen, and Schulz's longtime friend and attorney Edwin Anderson, progressed their dream to establish a permanent home for Schulz's artwork. Jean said, "I just wanted people to see his comic strips at their original size and not reduced to fit a newspaper's limited space."

CALIFORNIA COLLECTION

The Charles M. Schulz Museum and Research Center in Santa Rosa, California, opened in 2002. It houses the world's largest collection of the cartoonist's work,

MUSEUM BUILDING

With its subtle echoing of comic frames and the rounded forms of *Peanuts* characters, the Museum entrance welcomes visitors into Schulz's world. Schulz himself was involved in the museum's design until his death in 2000.

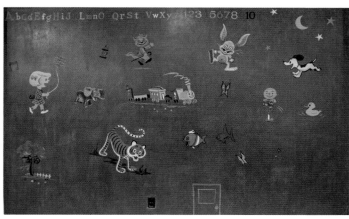

COMIC COLLECTION
The heart of the museum's collection is the nearly 7,000 original strip drawings on display, with work from 1950 to 2000.

as well as a re-creation of Schulz's art studio, and art installations by other artists, including the *Wrapped Snoopy House* artwork by conceptual artist Christo. The Museum has welcomed over one million visitors to its permanent and temporary exhibitions. Working closely with Jean Schulz, the museum's curators have highlighted fascinating and little-explored aspects of Schulz's career, from Schulz's love of Lewis Carroll's *Alice's Adventures in Wonderland* to his fondness for name-dropping his famous friends in the strip.

TOKYO SATELLITE
In December 2019, the Snoopy Museum Tokyo opened in Minami-machida Grandberry Park in Machida, Tokyo. The world's only satellite of the Schulz Museum, it exhibits original art, reproductions, and comic strips, as well as vintage goods and animation. Visitors can even make their own Snoopy plush dolls at special workshops!

MEREDITH'S MURAL
One of the museum's most cherished items is a mural that Schulz painted in 1951 at the family's Colorado Springs home for his daughter Meredith. Charlie Brown and Snoopy are featured along with the early character Patty, holding a balloon.

INSPIRED ARTWORK
Japanese artist Yoshiteru Otani created the 17 x 22 feet (5 x 7 m) mural that covers a wall of the museum's Great Hall. Depicting Lucy holding the football for Charlie Brown, it is made of 3,588 *Peanuts* comic strip images printed on individual 2-by-8-inch (5-by-20-cm) ceramic tiles.

SNOOPY IN JAPAN
At the Snoopy Museum Tokyo, visitors are welcomed by a 26-foot- (8-m-) long sleeping Snoopy in the Snoopy Room.

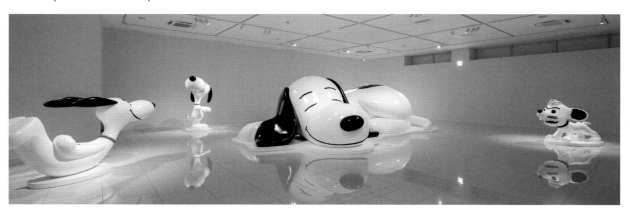

Modern Merchandise

Licensed partnerships for Charles M. Schulz's characters continue to find creative new ways to reinterpret the gang. Many fun toys come from Japan, including Snoopy and friends as peanut-shaped Coo'nuts from toy maker Bandai, which come in blind bags and wobble. The first series featured the key characters, while the second and third series delved deeper into the world of baseball and Snoopy's family, including some lesser-known characters such as Violet and Peggy Jean. Also from Japan, Medicom Toy creates collectible Bearbricks—here, Charlie Brown keeps his classic cartoon look with the addition of bear's ears, in a contemporary blend of styles. Perhaps most eye-catching of all is a life-size Snoopy created by San Francisco–based collectibles brand Super7. The 16-inch- (41-cm-) tall vinyl toy features the Charlie Brown mask and shirt that Snoopy wore in a strip from October 28, 1953. Back to the future indeed!

1 Snoopy figurine, Enesco LLC (2015) **2** Snoopy Wood Block Stacking Game, Hallmark (2014) **3** Classic Peanuts Character, Pigpen; Dark Horse (2009) **4** Miniature Snoopy, Coo'nuts (2019) **5** Great Pumpkin cookie jar, Kiddyland Limited Edition (2002) **6** Bearbrick Charlie Brown, Medicom (2016) **7** Faron plush toy, Nakajima Corporation (2018) **8** Mac Tools, Shirley Muldowney Lucy Dragster (2002) **9** Snoopy helmet, AXS Corporation (2013) **10** *Be More Snoopy*, DK (2020) **11** Coinpurse, StylingLife (2016) **12** Snoopy mug, Funko Pop (2015) **13** Snoopy toy, Super7 (2019) **14** Snoopy figurine, Danbury Mint (2008) **15** Kite-Eating Tree, Enesco LLC (2014)

New Horizons

Peanuts continues to be a worldwide phenomenon. In 2015, *The Peanuts Movie* (known in some countries as *Snoopy and Charlie Brown: A Peanuts Movie*) saw the gang back in a feature animation for the first time in 35 years—and, for the first time ever, on the big screen in 3D CGI animation, courtesy of Blue Sky Studios. Subsequent years have seen the gang just as busy, from helping to get young people out to vote with the Rock the Vote campaign in 2016 to a major *Peanuts* exhibition in London in 2018— showcasing original *Peanuts* strips alongside work from contemporary artists and designers inspired by Schulz's work.

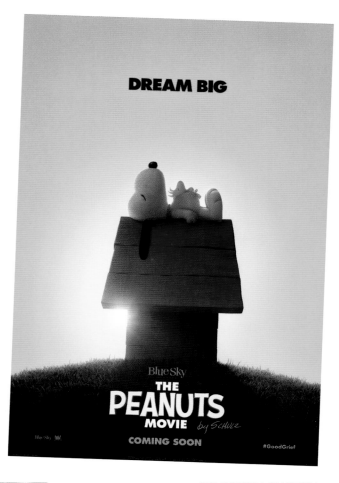

DREAM BIG

Blue Sky

THE PEANUTS MOVIE *by Schulz*

COMING SOON

#GoodGrief

BIG-SCREEN SNOOPY

Released in 2015, *The Peanuts Movie*—directed by Steve Martino from a screenplay by Schulz's son Craig, his grandson Bryan, and Cornelius Uliano—brought the strip's characters to life in fully realized computer-generated animation.

DRESSED TO IMPRESS

In *The Peanuts Movie*, Charlie Brown tries to impress the Little Red-Haired Girl, now given the name Heather Wold.

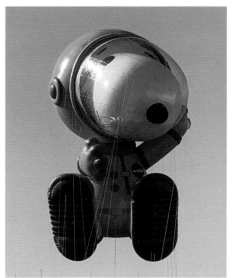

ASTRONAUT SNOOPY

The 93rd annual Macy's Thanksgiving Day Parade in 2019 saw Astronaut Snoopy take to the skies to celebrate the 50th anniversary of the moon landing.

SNOOPY IN SPACE

The 50th anniversary of *Peanuts'* association with NASA saw a new partnership with the space agency in 2019 to promote STEM to students. In the series *Snoopy in Space*, animated by Wildbrain Studios, Snoopy launched into space again—this time becoming a NASA astronaut and taking command of the International Space Station, as well as exploring the moon and beyond. The 12 episodes were preceded by a nine-minute documentary by Morgan Neville titled *Peanuts in Space: Secrets of Apollo 10*, starring Ron Howard and Jeff Goldblum. The crowds at Macy's Thanksgiving Day Parade that year were given further opportunity to see the space-bound beagle as an astronaut Snoopy balloon took flight above their heads! Snoopy's new animated adventures will also land him back home on Earth with *The Snoopy Show*, streaming on Apple TV+. What next, Charlie Brown?

SPACE HUG
In *Snoopy in Space*, the orbiting beagle is delighted to see a familiar face in space: his friend of friends, Woodstock.

DANCE PARTY
Snoopy and the gang show off their dance moves in *The Snoopy Show*, a new animated series streaming on Apple TV+.

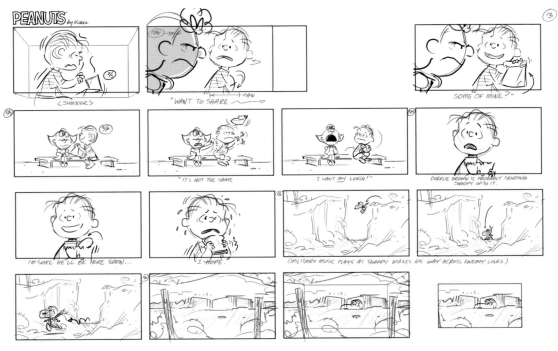

STORYBOARDS
A storyboard from *The Snoopy Show* features Snoopy as the Flying Ace sent on a daring mission to get Sally her school lunch!

Thank You, Charlie Brown!

Let's celebrate the gang—70 years old and still going strong! Few—if any—other strips have attained the broad cultural and global impact of *Peanuts* or its enduring appeal. The strip's emotional intelligence and warm but biting humor is every bit as reassuring today as it was during the tumultuous times Schulz lived in. Many of its themes—loneliness, fear of failure, mental health, body image, gender inequality—continue to resonate. His characters are honest in a way that feels modern. They don't pretend to have perfect lives. They are authentic. Whether it's Charlie Brown's neuroticism, Lucy's pitiless drive, Linus's thoughtfulness, Schroeder's obsessiveness, Peppermint Patty's individuality, Marcie's overachievement, Sally's underachievement, or Snoopy's extraversion—There's a place for everyone in Schulz's inclusive world. Long may it continue!

"Having a large audience does not, of course, prove that something is necessarily good, and I subscribe to the theory that only a creation that speaks to succeeding generations can truly be labeled art."

—Charles M. Schulz

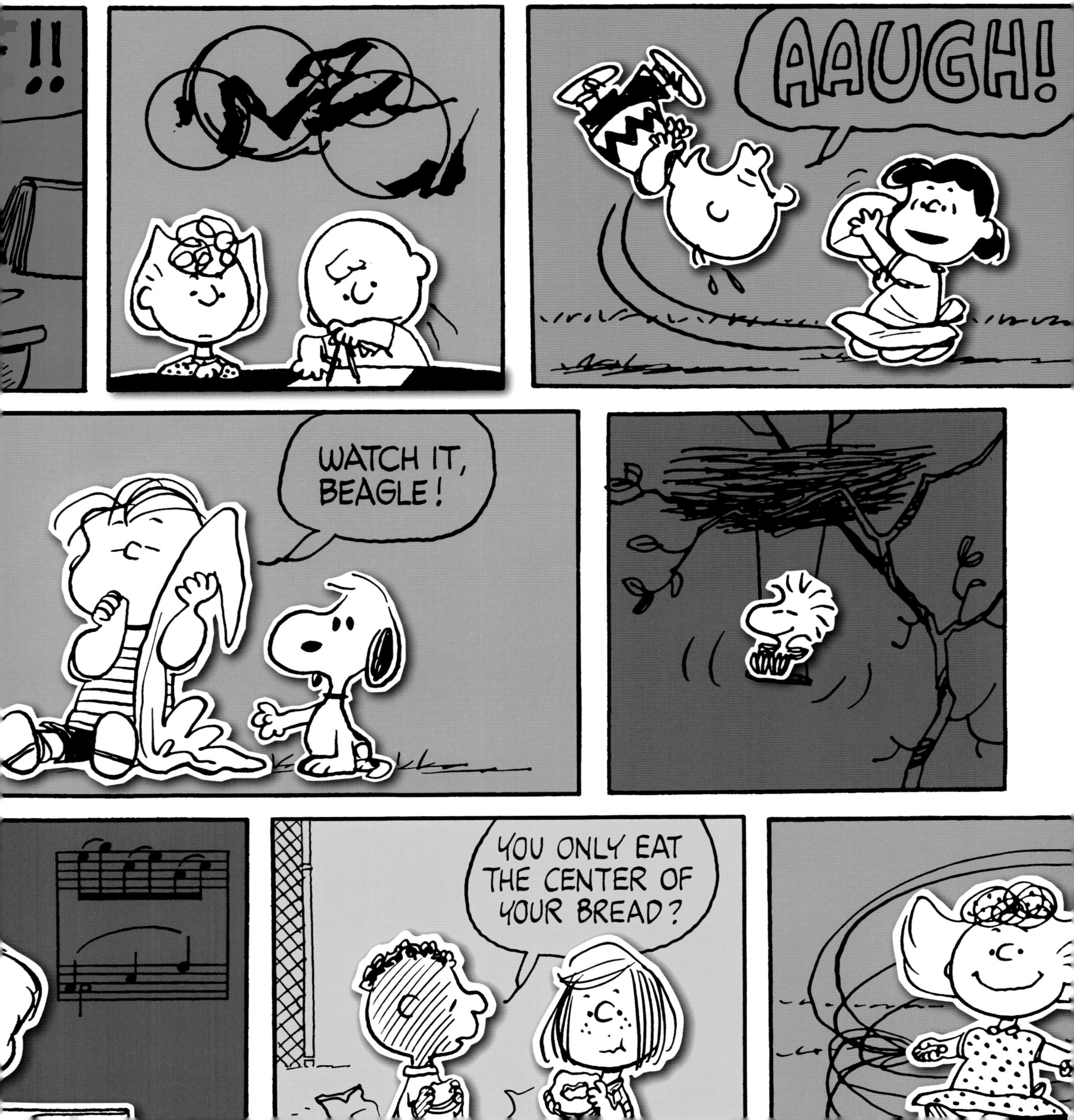
AAUGH!
WATCH IT, BEAGLE!
YOU ONLY EAT THE CENTER OF YOUR BREAD?

Index

Page numbers in **bold** refer to main entries

K

L

M

N

O

P

R

S

Picture Credits

The publisher would like to thank the following for their kind permission to reproduce their images:

(Key: a-above; b-below/bottom; c-centre; f-far; l-left; r-right; t-top; CMSM-Charles M. Schulz Museum and Research Center; PWW-Peanuts Worldwide; SFIPT-Schulz Family Intellectual Property Trust)

1 CMSM: CMSM (cb). 2 CMSM: PWW / Schmid Bros. / ANRI. 4 CMSM: PWW (cb, crb, bc); PWW / Crosley (cra); PWW / Simon Simple (ca). 5 CMSM: Public Domain / PWW (c); PWW / Snoopy Museum Tokyo (cra); PWW / Dark Horse (br); Snoopy Museum Tokyo (ftl, tl, tc, tr, ftr). 8 Getty Images: Bettmann / Contributor. 9 CMSM: Gakken (bl). 11 CMSM: SFIPT (clb). 12 CMSM: SFIPT (c). 13 CMSM: PWW (bl); SFIPT (crb). 14 CMSM: PWW (r); SFIPT (bc). 15 CMSM: Mendelson Productions (tc); PWW (cb, c/1967); PWW / Modern Toys (unlicensed) (br); State of California (cr). 16 CMSM: City of Los Angeles / PWW (cl); PWW / Simon Simple (bl). 17 CMSM: PWW / Holt, Rinehart, & Winston (tr). 18 CMSM: CMSM / National Cartoonists Society (cl). Getty Images: Los Angeles Examiner / University of Southern California / Contributor / Corbis (bc). 19 CMSM: PWW (tc); SFIPT (tr). 21 Alamy Stock Photo: Jim West (tr). CMSM: CMSM / Public Domain (c); SFIPT (tl). 22-23 Shutterstock.com: Here (Background). 24 CMSM: Barney Google & Snuffy Smith © King Features Syndicate Inc., World Rights Reserved. (br); SFIPT (tr, cl). 25 CMSM: SFIPT (cra, br, cl). 26 CMSM: SFIPT. 27 CMSM: SFIPT (br). 28 CMSM: SFIPT (tr, bl, bc). 29 CMSM: SFIPT (bc, crb, cra, tl). 30 CMSM: Public Domain (tl). Shutterstock.com: Mega Pixel (b/Background). 31 CMSM: PWW (r). 34 CMSM: CMSM. 35 CMSM: SFIPT (tr, br); SFIPT (clb). 36 Getty Images: Bettmann / Contributor (tl). 38-39 CMSM: PWW / San Francisco Chronicle. Shutterstock.com: Here (Background). 41 CMSM: SFIPT (tr). 42 CMSM: PWW (crb); SFIPT (br). 43 Library of Congress, Washington, D.C.: (br). Shutterstock.com: Mega Pixel (clb/Background). 45 Shutterstock.com: Mega Pixel (b/Background). 48 CMSM: SFIPT (tr). 49 CMSM: PWW (br); SFIPT (tc); PWW / Schmid Bros (bl). 53 Shutterstock.com: Mega Pixel (br). 54 Shutterstock.com: Mega Pixel (t). 55 CMSM: PWW / Fantasy Records (tc, tr). 56 CMSM: PWW (clb). 66 Library of Congress, Washington, D.C.: Estate of Charles M. Schulz. (br). 70-71 CMSM: PWW. 72 CMSM: PWW (tr); SFIPT (crb, bl). 73 CMSM: SFIPT (tr); PWW / Fantagraphics (tc). 74-75 Shutterstock.com: Here (Background). 76 CMSM: PWW (tr, cra, cl, c, cr). 77 CMSM: PWW (tr, cla, clb, cb, cb/Bonjour, br); PWW / Twin Vision / American Brotherhood for the Blind (cr); PWW / / Twin Vision / American Brotherhood for the Blind (cl); PWW / Tivola Publishing (tc). 79 CMSM: CMSM (c); PWW / Mattel (tl). 89 CMSM: Bradford Exchange (tr); PWW / Hallmark (bl, cb). 93 CMSM: City of Los Angeles / PWW (bl). 94 CMSM: PWW (crb); PWW / Hallmark (bl). 95 CMSM: PWW (tl, tc, tr, bl, br). 97 CMSM: SFIPT (cra). 98 CMSM: PWW (tc). 99 CMSM: PWW (cl, c, cr, crb, tl, tr). 100 CMSM: CMSM / National Cartoonists Society (r); SFIPT (bl). 101 CMSM: City and County of San Francisco (tl); CMSM / Public Domain (tr); CMSM / National Cartoonists Society (br); State of California (bl). 102 Shutterstock.com: Mega Pixel (ca/Background). 105 CMSM: PWW / Schmid Bros. (tr). 107 CMSM: E.M.I. Records (cla); PWW / Hallmark (clb); PWW (br, clb/Snoopy). 108 Shutterstock.com: Mega Pixel (t/Background). 109 CMSM: PWW / / Schmid, Co. (cl); PWW / Department 56 (crb); PWW / Schmid, Co. (c); PWW / Danbury Mint (b). 113 Shutterstock.com: Mega Pixel (b). 116-117 CMSM: CMSM (cb). 119 CMSM: PWW / Hallmark (cr). 124 CMSM: PWW (bc, br); PWW / AVON Products (clb, fcl, ca, ca/Comb Case, cla, cla/Shampoo Box); PWW / Selchow & Righter Co. (cra); PWW / Simon Simple (bl). 125 CMSM: PWW (bl, tr, c/Easter Beagle, cl, fcl); PWW / Mattel (cr); PWW / King Seeley Thermos (tl, tc); PWW / J.Chein and Co. (cb); PWW / Hallmark (bc); PWW / Simon Simple (crb/All Buttons). 126 CMSM: PWW (b); Schmid, Co. (c). 127 CMSM: Mendelson Productions (tl, cra); PWW (cb, crb). 128 CMSM: SFIPT (tr); Snoopy's Home Ice (b). 129 CMSM: Snoopy's Home Ice / DJ Ashton (tl); PWW (bc, br). 131 CMSM: NASA (tc); PWW / Schmid Bros (tl). NASA: (br). 132-133 CMSM: PWW. Shutterstock.com: Here (Background). 135 CMSM: CMSM (c, cr). 137 CMSM: PWW (cra). Shutterstock.com: Mega Pixel (b/Background). 139 CMSM: PWW / Ideal Toy Company (tl). 143 CMSM: PWW / Dark Horse (cb). 147 Shutterstock.com: Mega Pixel (br). 151 CMSM: PWW (cb). 152 Shutterstock.com: Mega Pixel (t/Background). 153 CMSM: PWW (br). 155 CMSM: © Christo 2003. 156 CMSM: PWW (tr). 157 CMSM: PWW / Garcia. Shutterstock.com: Mega Pixel (r/Background). 158 Shutterstock.com: Mega Pixel (clb/Background). 161 CMSM: SFIPT (cr). 163 CMSM: PWW (cra). 166-167 Shutterstock.com: Here (Background). 168 Shutterstock.com: Mega Pixel (t/Background). 171 CMSM: PWW (cb). Shutterstock.com: Mega Pixel (br/Background). 172 CMSM: PWW / John Knox Press (tl). 174 CMSM: PWW (cl, cr). 175 CMSM: PWW (tl, cra, b). 177 Shutterstock.com: Mega Pixel (t/Background). 178 CMSM: PWW (cr, bl, cb); PWW / McDonald's (br/All Glasses); PWW / PEZ Candy Inc. (tr/All Figures). 179 CMSM: PWW (clb, crb/All Figurines); Nintendo / PWW (br); PWW / Playskool (cra); PWW / International Trading Technology (tl); PWW / Schmid, Co. (cb); PWW / AVIVA, Inc. (tc); PWW / Disneyland / Vista Records (cl, c). 182 CMSM: Tim Menees, Pittsburgh Post Gazette (cra). 183 CMSM: Cathy Guisewite, Universarl Press Syndicate (tr); Mike Luckovich, Atlanta Constitution (tl); Stan Lee, Marvel Comics (cl); Patrick McDonnell, King Features Syndicate (cra); Steve Kelley, San Diego Union Tribune / Copley New Service (clb); Mike Thompson, Detroit Free Press (br). 184-185 Shutterstock.com: Here (Background). 186 CMSM: Macy's (tr, b). 187 123RF.com: guo zhonghua (cla). CMSM: PWW (crb, bl, bc); PWW / Cedar Fair Entertainment Company (tl). Getty Images: Los Angeles Examiner / University of Southern California / Contributor / Corbis (tr). 188 CMSM: CMSM. 189 CMSM: CMSM (tr, tl, crb); PWW (b). 190 CMSM: PWW / Enesco LLC (tc); PWW / Coo'nuts (cb); PWW / Dark Horse (clb); PWW / Kiddyland (bl); PWW / Medicom (bc); PWW / Hallmark (tr); PWW / Nakajima Corporation (crb). 190-191 CMSM: PWW / MAC Tools (bc). 191 CMSM: PWW / AXS Corporation (tl); PWW / StylingLife (tr); PWW / Funko POP (cla); PWW / Danbury Mint (cra); PWW / Enesco LLC (clb); PWW / Super7 (c). 192 Hannah Guy Casey: (br). 193 PWW: WildBrain (tr, cr, b). 199 CMSM: Sanrio (b)

Cover images: *Front:* **CMSM:** Determined Productions br, PWW cla, PWW / Simon Simple clb; *Back:* **CMSM:** Modern Toys tl, PWW cla, PWW / International Trading Technology clb, PWW / J.Chein and Co. cra, PWW / PEZ Candy Inc. cb, PWW / Simon Simple tc

Endpaper images: *Front:* **CMSM:** PWW / San Francisco Chronicle ; *Back:* **CMSM:** St. Petersburg Times (FL) ;

Snoopy in Space and The Snoopy Show is © 2019 DHX-Peanuts Productions Inc., a WildBrain Company, and © 2020 DHX-Peanuts Productions Inc., a WildBrain Company, respectively.

All other images © Peanuts

Bibliography

Derrick Bang, *50 Years of Happiness: A Tribute to Charles M. Schulz* (Charles M. Schulz Museum, 1999);
Derrick Bang, *Charles M. Schulz: Li'l Beginnings* (Charles M. Schulz Museum, 2003);
Andrew Farago, *The Complete Peanuts Family Album* (Weldon Owen, 2017);
Nat Gertler, *The Snoopy Treasures* (Thunder Bay Press, 2015);
Chip Kidd, *Only What's Necessary: Charles M. Schulz and the Art of Peanuts* (Abrams, 2015);
David Michaelis, *Schulz and Peanuts: A Biography* (HarperCollins, 2007);
Pamela J. Podger, "Christo wraps a doghouse", The San Francisco Chronicle, 11 Oct, 2003
Peggy Whitman Prenshaw, *More Conversations with Eudora Welty* (University Press of Mississippi, 1996);
Charles M. Schulz, *Celebrating Peanuts* (Andrews McMeel Publishing, 2015);
Charles M. Schulz, *Peanuts: A Golden Celebration* (HarperCollins, 1999);
Charles M. Schulz, *Peanuts Jubilee: My Life and Art with Charlie Brown and Others* (Holt, Rinehart & Winston, 1975);
Charles M. Schulz (ed. Gary Groth), *The Complete Peanuts: Volumes 1-26* (Fantagraphics, 2004-16)
Monte Schulz, "Regarding Schulz and Peanuts", The Comics Journal, No. 290, May 2008
Robert L. Short, *The Gospel According to Peanuts* (Harper & Row, 1968);
Benjamin Svetkey, "Peanuts' Girl Power Icons: How Charles M. Schulz's Comic Champions Feminism", Hollywood Reporter, Jan 4, 2016

OLAF ANDY BELLE SNOOPY MARBLES SPIKE

Senior Editor Emma Grange
Senior Art Editor Clive Savage
Picture Research Sumedha Chopra and Martin Copeland
Senior Production Editor Jennifer Murray
Senior Production Controller Louise Daly
Managing Editor Sarah Harland
Managing Art Editor Vicky Short
Publisher Julie Ferris
Art Director Lisa Lanzarini
Publishing Director Mark Searle

CAMERON + COMPANY
Publisher Chris Gruener
Creative Director Iain R. Morris
Art Director Suzi Hutsell
Assistant Designers Amy Wheless, Rob Dolgaard, Emily Studer
Managing Editor Jan Hughes
Editorial Assistant Mason Harper

First American Edition, 2020
Published in the United States by DK Publishing
1450 Broadway, Suite 801, New York, NY 10018

Page design copyright © 2020 Dorling Kindersley Limited
DK, a Division of Penguin Random House LLC
20 21 22 23 24 10 9 8 7 6 5 4 3 2 1
001–316401–Sep/2020

PEANUTS

A catalog record for this book is available from the Library of Congress.
ISBN 978-1-4654-9785-7

Printed in China

DK books are available at special discounts when purchased in bulk for sales promotions,
premiums, fund-raising, or educational use. For details, contact: DK Publishing Special Markets,
1450 Broadway, Suite 801, New York, NY 10018
SpecialSales@dk.com

ACKNOWLEDGMENTS
DK would like to thank Simon Beecroft for his text and expertise; Craig Herman
at Peanuts Worldwide; Alexis Fajardo and Alena Carnes of Charles M. Schulz Creative
Associates; Sarah Breaux, Dinah Houghtaling, Benjamin Peery, Benjamin Clark,
and Karen Johnson from the Charles M. Schulz Museum and Research Center;
Deborah Wilson for photography; and Nat Gertler for fact checking.

For the curious
www.dk.com
www.peanuts.com

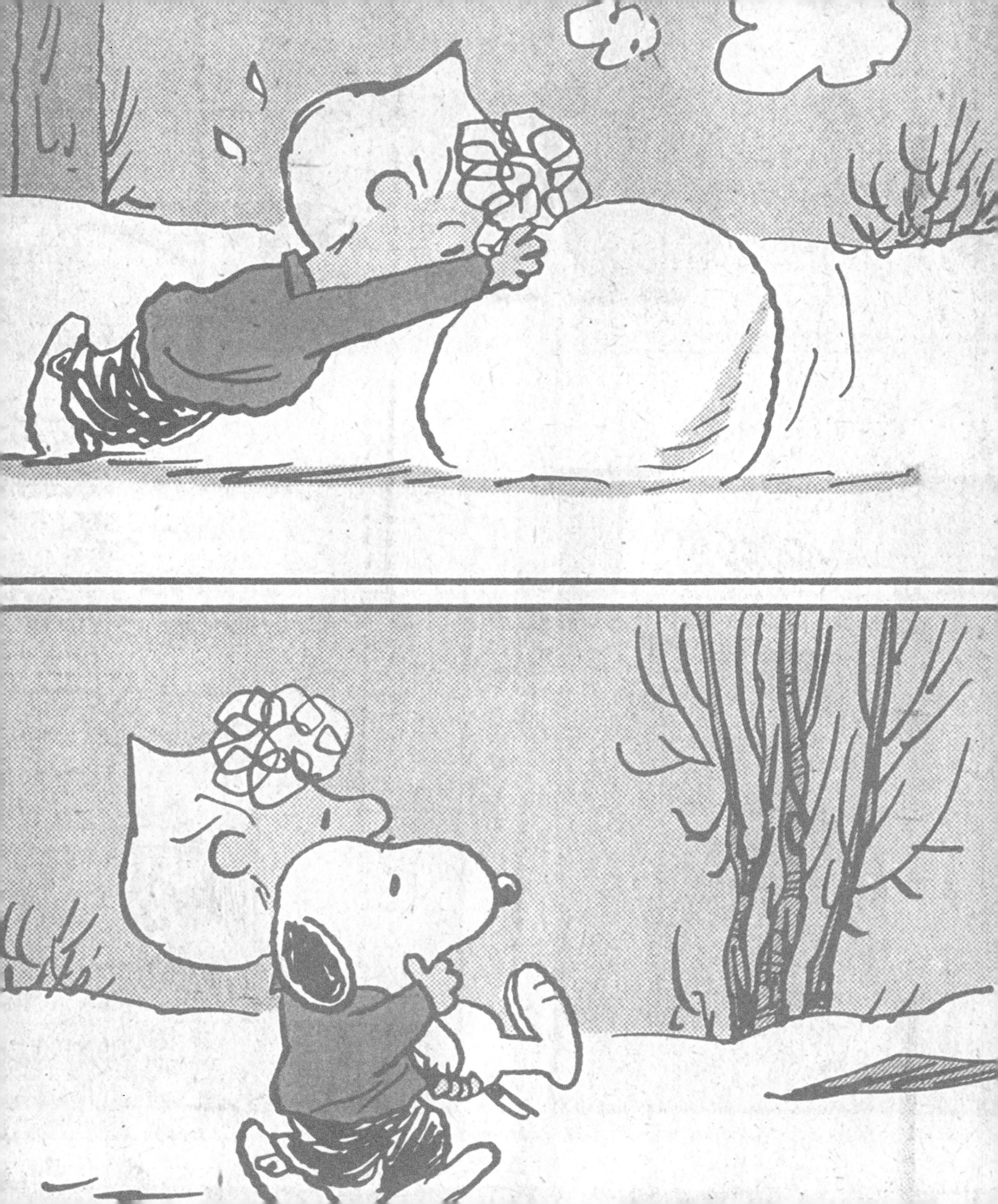